Florian Malzacher, *The Art of Assembly*

Florian Malzacher is a curator, author, and dramaturg as well as the host of *The Art of Assembly*, a series of talks and conversations about the potential of gathering in art, activism, and politics. From 2006–2012 he was festival programmer of the interdisciplinary festival steirischer herbst in Graz; from 2013–2017 the artistic director of the Impulse Theater Festival. He is the editor of numerous publications on theatre, on the relationship between art, activism, and politics, and on performance curation. These include (co)edited books on the work of theatre companies Forced Entertainment, Rimini Protokoll, and Nature Theater of Oklahoma, as well as *Truth is Concrete: A Handbook for Artistic Strategies in Real Politics* (2014), *Not Just a Mirror: Looking for the Political Theatre of Today* (2015) and *Empty Stages, Crowded Flats: Performativity as Curatorial Strategy* (2017). His books and essays have been translated into fifteen languages.

Florian Malzacher

THE ART OF ASSEMBLY

Political Theatre Today

Translated from the German
by Cory Tamler

Alexander Verlag Berlin
Martin E. Segal Theatre Center

© by Alexander Verlag Berlin 2023
Alexander Wewerka, Fredericiastr. 8, D–14050 Berlin
www.alexander-verlag.com | info@alexander-verlag.com
All rights reserved

Translation: Cory Tamler
Copy editing: Valerie Saint-Rossy, Marion Storm
Typesetting/Layout/Cover: Antje Wewerka
Printing and binding: lulu.com
ISBN 978-1-953892-13-3

CONTENTS

9   **Prologue**

19   **Representation**
26   Crises of Representation
27   *Regietheater* and Early Postdramatic Theatre
36   Politics and the Political
39   Anthropocene, Animism, and Posthumanism
42   Trembling Androids, Sweating Avatars

47   **Identity Politics**
49   Infiltrated Terms and Special Interests
56   Privileges and Unproductive Silences
58   Offended Offenders
60   Stumbling and Stuttering

63   **Participation**
68   Care and Confrontation
75   Safer Spaces, Braver Spaces
80   Participation Behind the Scenes
83   Immersion: Participation as Submission

89   **Art and Activism**
97   Means and Ends
99   Fake News
103   Forced Positionings

109	**Theatre as Assembly**
110	Performative Assemblies
113	Parliaments, Summits, Courtrooms
122	Pre-enactments
129	Assembling Knowledge
131	When Realism Becomes Reality
137	**Epilogue**
140	Notes
151	Index of Names
154	Image Credits
155	Acknowledgments

"Art is not a mirror that reflects reality,
but a hammer with which it can be shaped."
(Marx, Brecht, or Mayakovsky)[1]

Christoph Schlingensief: *Please Love Austria!* (Montage)

PROLOGUE

Some protesters, red-faced, scream at one another. Others try to convince the numerous onlookers in strident tones: their country is being overrun by strangers; their culture, their families, their identity all are in grave danger. An old man, eyes brimming with tears, waves a tabloid featuring his fears—front page, capital letters. A handful of Korean tourists observe the strange spectacle, confused: "Little Austria" against the rest of the world.

More than twenty years have passed since the late German film- and theatremaker Christoph Schlingensief dropped his shipping containers housing *Please Love Austria!* (2000) in the center of Vienna, right next to the famous opera house. The conservative Chancellor Wolfgang Schüssel had just concluded his devil's pact with right-wing demagogue Jörg Haider and the Freedom Party of Austria (FPÖ). Other EU countries were discussing sanctions against the fellow member state, and Austria itself was discussing the borders defining the country, the borders defining democracy, and the borders defining art. The world was watching.

It was against this backdrop that Schlingensief staged his long since legendary production under the striking banner "Foreigners out!"—a reality show with real asylum seekers. For six days, the containers were home to a group of immigrants who could be observed around the clock (via an online platform connected to surveillance cameras) as they went about their lives, while the Austrian population was invited to vote them out of the country one after the other.

Prologue

The scandal was enormous. Conservatives felt defamed by the parody of their own arguments; leftists were angered by what was, in their view, a cynical display of human suffering coupled with willful ignorance of years of activist work on the ground, which the spectacle made more difficult. It was the year of the first German-language installment of the reality television show *Big Brother*, which some riled-up feuilleton commentators heralded as nothing less than the beginning of the end of the humanist age.

That was a long time ago. The same television show is still running, but although it was once controversial, now it seems a little old-fashioned compared to all the other reality programs which are at least as cynical. In Austria, the FPÖ, despite numerous (at times grotesque) scandals, remained a prominent fixture and for a while even managed to instate party members as Ministers of the Interior, Foreign Affairs, and Defense—and even as Vice Chancellor. This is no exceptional case. Far-right parties are part of parliamentary everyday life all over the world, and it is not only in Hungary and Poland that constitutional states are being transformed into "illiberal democracies." *Please Love Austria!* stayed playful in spite of serious opposition and even impassioned aggression. Schlingensief succeeded in walking a very thin line that stumped almost every attempt to pin down his intentions—unlikely that all this would still be possible today. Political and social, but also artistic conflicts have ossified and taken on sharper edges; the world has become so confusing that it does not seem to need art to create space for ambiguity. The storming of the Capitol in Washington, D.C. in 2021 is just one recent example of the many images of political escalation that have long since eclipsed even Schlingensief's imagination. Supposedly clear lines of conflict around identity, nationalism, racism, colonialism, climate catastrophes, social tensions, and other issues have split open, becoming deep, apparently insurmountable rifts.

> **The world has become so confusing that it does not seem to need art to create space for ambiguity.**

Prologue

In some respects, the West, along with large parts of the East, still suffers from the aftereffects of TINA ("There is no alternative"), the much-quoted doctrine with which the British Prime Minister Margaret Thatcher legitimized her devastating social cutbacks at the beginning of the 1980s: an early star of that neoliberalism which, despite altered rhetoric, has lost little of its power to this day and has long since deeply inscribed itself in economic, social, and political structures.

In 1989, the Berlin Wall dividing Europe fell: the Socialist system in the East collapsed parallel to the abandoning of the welfare state in the West. At the end of the 1990s, the "Third Way" of British Prime Minister Tony Blair and German Chancellor Gerhard Schröder brought social democracy onto the more market-oriented course of the "new center" which was becoming an effective doctrine in many other countries. "No alternative" became a central concept, and with it, much open political competition fell by the wayside. As early as 1992, political scientist Francis Fukuyama provided a kind of historical-philosophical legitimation of TINA in his book *The End of History*: after the collapse of the Eastern bloc and with it, of communist ideology, for him the liberal market economy and parliamentary democracy were the unstoppable victors.[2] No need to argue anymore …

But history was not over after all, and we still feel the side effects of TINA and the like today. They have prepared the social ground for a state of affairs in which the absence of alternatives is regarded as common sense and, as theorists from Chantal Mouffe to Slavoj Žižek remark, political values have been replaced by moral ones.

The fact that in recent years, political and social positions have become increasingly radical and opposing opinions more and more irreconcilable is, like the accompanying triumphal marches of right-wing and far-right parties, not a contradiction to our TINA-society but rather its direct consequence. The denial or demonization of possible political alternatives as a kind of political consensus blackmail is one of the reasons for the radicalization of opinions, especially at the right end of the spectrum. So now there are two sides, both of which can see no alternatives to their own solutions.

Ironically, the heralding of the "end of history" is the perfidious variant of a social model for which many leftist or liberal philosophers—from Karl Marx to Jürgen Habermas or John Rawls—have wished: a model of unification based on the premise that rational considerations will one day lead people to overcome their own individual interests and agree on the right thing.

But we are not particularly reasonable beings. Feelings and selfish considerations too will always play a role. Nor is there for some conflicts, as Chantal Mouffe emphasizes, simply *one* rational solution. There will never be a world without power structures and particular interests: "[W]hile we desire an end to conflict, if we want people to be free we must always allow for the possibility that conflict may appear and to provide an arena where differences can be confronted. The democratic process should supply that arena."[3]

Mouffe's concept of *agonistic pluralism* therefore describes democracy as a battlefield in which we must have the opportunity to act out our differences as opponents without resolving them. This demand is not easy to digest, because it not only contradicts any hope for democracy as a comprehensive safe space, it also goes far beyond the argument that competition enlivens business: "Adversaries do fight—even fiercely but according to a shared set of rules, and their positions, despite being ultimately irreconcilable, are accepted as legitimate perspectives."[4] The readiness for such acceptance is the only way we can prevent an *ant*agonism from coming to pass, one that puts an end to all negotiation and understanding and whose final consequence is (real or at least symbolic) civil war: a situation that seems to have been almost achieved in many countries such as the USA or Brazil. "We could say that the task of democracy is to transform antagonism into agonism."[5] For

Christoph Schlingensief: *Please Love Austria!*

Prologue

democracy must always be reestablished and negotiated; it lives on accepted conflict and partisanship.

Which opinions do we allow, and to which do we want to deny space? Which conflicts can the theatre portray, and about which ones should it remain silent? In a time when, on the one hand, George W. Bush's dictum "If you're not with us, you're against us"—radicalized by Donald Trump—is experiencing an astonishing renaissance on all sides of the political spectrum, and on the other hand, the logic of consensus is still trying to put many democratic discussions to bed, theatre can be a space in which a playful (but serious) agonism not only keeps contradictions alive, but above all allows them to be articulated freely. After all, it is no coincidence that Mouffe's concept takes its name from ancient sport and culture tournaments. *Agon* is also the name of the contest between opposing arguments in Greek tragedy.

> **Theatre can be a space in which a playful (but serious) agonism not only keeps contradictions alive, but above all allows them to be articulated freely.**

Western theatre always was above all a medium for the representation of conflicts and opposites: between good and evil, between ideas and ideologies, societies and nations, powers and the powerful, ideals and traditions, between generations, families, and couples, or even within the psyche of an individual person. The conflicts that are carried out are representative, sometimes physical, sometimes psychological, sometimes discursive. Theatre is a place of negotiation, a space of (albeit often partisan) agonistic pluralism, however often last acts may suggest a reassuring conclusion.

Alarming as the current social, ecological, and political situation is, for the theatre it also offers an opportunity to spark new social imagination, either in collaboration or in friction with the numerous movements around the world. How can other forms of coexistence be thought, tried out, discussed, and confronted together in the theatre? How can theatre participate in thinking about the society and the world we actually want? How can theatre, without resorting to cheap preaching and didacticism, dare to attempt—together with its audience—confident answers? What forms, both aesthetic and ethical, are needed in order to be truly political and not just to perform a political attitude?

A look at the current international theatre scene shows that there is a strong desire among artists and audiences for a theatre that not only addresses pressing political issues, but itself becomes a public space in which aesthetics and ethics are not contradictory. A theatre that is—how deceptively simple this seems—political both in its content and in its form.

This book is an attempt to understand how theatre today can be a concrete place where the world around us—political events, social visions, major struggles, and pragmatic attempts at solutions—is not only shown, but consciously shaped. And to understand where, in this work, artistic and political dangers might lurk.

This foray through political theatre does not claim to be complete. On the contrary, it is largely based on my own direct encounters and experiences as an audience member, and not infrequently on my participation in projects as a curator, dramaturg, or co-initiator. Therefore, there are points of particular emphasis, digressions, and blind spots. Although artists from many parts of the world play an essential role in this book, there is a focus on the German-speaking world. And on so-called postdramatic theatre, which is in turn internationally entangled in many ways and continuously interacts with artistic works and discourses from a wide variety of regions.

Thus, this book does not even attempt a comprehensive presentation of everything that could currently be understood as political theatre. Much that fills the feuilletons is not discussed here. It is a partisan book. At the same time, it is a searching book, written about a searching theatre within a searching society. Where it

Prologue

offers answers, they are provisional, just as theatre itself is always provisional. What works and is important today will be outdated tomorrow, at best a precursor for the next step, at worst a dead end. But at the same time, that's exactly what political theatre is all about: countering an often supposedly well-founded relativism with serious, consistent assertions, and at the same time knowing that these are always only working theses. All examples in this book can only be understood in the context of their time, and of the geographical setting in which they emerge.

Sometimes a year or one hundred kilometers' distance can change the whole picture.

Part of the necessary background is that this book was written before the outbreak of the COVID-19 virus. It appeared in its original German-language edition right at the beginning of the first lockdown, at a time when almost no performance could be shown anywhere. It is not yet possible to foresee the long-term consequences this will have for theatre.

> In the paradoxical machine of theatre everything is simultaneously actual and fictional, real and symbolic. You can play along, be right in the middle of it, and at the same time observe yourself from the outside.

The playwright Heiner Müller once called for all theatres in the world to be closed for a year so that we could see what we really need them for.[6] Now, venues and festivals were shut down in actuality around the globe again and again for months and months. But instead of fundamentally rethinking their own medium and its routines, theatre artists engaged in constant activity. Streamings and discussions, readings, lectures, Zoom performances ... . Theatres were closed almost worldwide and yet there was more theatre available every day than anyone could possibly watch. The horror vacui was too strong. It prevented almost any silence; it prevented us from taking almost any time to reevaluate our art and our lives. As if we were afraid that the moment we stopped, everything would fall apart forever.

But this never-ending talking and doing contained a hidden answer to Heiner Müller. While the phantom pain grew, it became more and more clear that all the screening and Zooming was not even close to the real thing. It was a permanent reference to something absent. To something that used to be there and hopefully would be there again soon. It only existed in this relationship.

In this spirit the works described in this book are *Gesellschaftsspiele* (parlor games) that can only be played collectively. The double meaning of the German term (literally translating to "society games"), which is also the title of the original edition, brings a larger social dimension into view.

The rules of these games can often only be understood through playing them; sometimes they are not easy to figure out. But as much as you may get caught up in the game, it is always about keeping an eye on what is at stake. On what basis is the game played? Who made the rules and to what extent do they determine what is played and who can play?

These games take place in the paradoxical machine of theatre, where everything is simultaneously actual and fictional, real and symbolic. You can play along, be right in the middle of it, and at the same time observe yourself from the outside. Theatre is always a social, but also a self-reflexive practice. Political theatre makes use of exactly that.

Anta Helena Recke: *Mittelreich*

REPRESENTATION

A family sits at a table. An average family that has made something of itself. That has something to lose and not much to gain. It is a story of war, rape, loneliness, fear, but also quite mundanely one of average prosperity and the fear of loss of status, of fathers who are dominant yet cowardly, of silence and avoiding responsibility. A story that could take place anywhere. And that is, at the same time, deeply rooted in German collective consciousness; a postwar narrative hearkening back to when psychological repression became a national virtue. Harsh, yet steeped in melancholy framed by Brahms' *German Requiem*, the banal nestles up to the transcendental: "For all flesh is as grass / And all the glory of man / as the flower of the grass. / The grass withers / And its flower falls away."[7] But something is off in this picture staged in a barren, somehow at once massive and claustrophobic hall. The family around the table is Black: an image average Germans recognize from American TV series, but not Bavarian family sagas.

In a country in which Black people in theatre appear almost exclusively as *explicitly* Black people (which is why Black actors end up playing not only the same types, but also often exactly the same roles, over and over), director Anta Helena Recke has bootlegged the already existing production *Mittelreich* (2015)[8] by Anna-Sophie Mahler on the main stage of the Münchner Kammerspiele. One to one—the same stage design, the same text, the same movements, the same sequence of events—only the actors, the choir, the musicians have been replaced by Black protagonists. It is an imitation in the tradition of US-American appropriation artists such as Elaine Sturtevant and Sherrie Levine, who since the 1970s have played a refined, often feminist or institutionally critical game with the male-dominated art world by repainting, reproducing, re-enacting, or otherwise appropriating well-known images.

But this *Mittelreich* copy (2017) is more than just a fairly exact appropriation of another director's staging. Through the appropriation of white figures (and their embodiment via white performers) by Black actors, it not only points out that Black bodies and stories are underrepresented on German stages if they appear at all. The work at the same time addresses a completely different, and ambivalent, appropriation: the dream, or the nightmare, of complete assimilation. A Black family that seems to have suppressed all nonwhite cultural influences, for example when the son wrestles with the fact that he does not know "what the German Wehrmacht soldier in Russia and France, who was my father, did." (The director herself writes that in this moment, she can't help but think of her Senegalese grandfather, "who distributed candy to German children as a French soldier after the war in Berlin."[9])

Along with the very clear demand for more visibility of people of color in artworks and in society, it is the profound ambiguity of this work that challenges the audience. The staging is not limited to the stage. Like any good work of appropriation art, it continuously refers to its contexts. To the white spectators, for example, who find themselves in a situation in which there is no clear right or wrong. One's own interpretation must be continually reinterpreted: Isn't personal worldly openness in fact paternalistic benevolence? Do we assess family power structures differently depending on whether we are watching a white or a Black family? What shifts when we realize that the refugees spoken about on stage—displaced Germans from the East after the Second World War—were just as unwelcome as refugees from Syria almost seventy years later? ("They are simply completely different people, these refugees. They just don't fit in here."[10]) And isn't it true that we (the white audience) can't help associating these thoughts with the actors on stage—even though they, like the director, were all born in Germany? And if, on the other hand, we believe ourselves to be truly "color blind" (or to have become "color blind" in the wake of the performance), are we not simply and self-reassuringly ignoring a difference that we, at least structurally, are maintaining ourselves? The partly fumbling, sometimes awkward—often "overly polite"[11] (Recke)—tone of the post show talkbacks says a lot about how difficult it still is for the German society to speak about discrimination at least in the public sphere.

But even if the dilemma of the white spectators is an essential part of the staging, the evening is at least as much directed at the people of color in the unusually mixed audience, because it offers possibilities for identification that are otherwise almost always absent in German municipal theatres.

Mittelreich is also one of surprisingly few examples of institutional critique in theatre. (This too being a genre of the visual arts, in which the criticism of an art institution becomes the actual artistic practice, usually commissioned by the very institution being criticized.) It was not only the producing theatre itself that was thrown into question by the fact that the cast had to be completely made up of guest actors because the ensemble had no Black members. *Mittelreich* is above all a clear critique of a concept of a repertoire as such that, as Recke says, almost always imagines a white audience—and at the same time considers this audience to be universal.[12] There are not many theatres that make the public investigation of their own actions part of their program.

Beyond this, the wider European theatre scene, the selection criteria for acting schools, ensembles, and repertoires, and not least the field of professional criticism with its quality categories are under scrutiny. While most of the reviews appreciated *Mittelreich*'s approach (and the work was invited to the Berlin Theatertreffen by a jury of critics), there were also absurd derailments. Under the headline "Black alone is not enough," the reviewer for the *Süddeutsche Zeitung*, one of the most important German daily papers, expressed her disappointment that the Black cast did not infuse the stale original production with a "reviving blood supply" as she had hoped (and explained coquettishly that—aren't we still allowed to say that?—this was of course "politically incorrect, because it was driven by, albeit positive, prejudices"). But maybe the actors simply weren't Black enough—because "they're not that Black, these six new bodies and faces." The actual discrimination would therefore not lie in the theatre system, but in this "altogether bad amateur theatre."[13]

Anta Helena Recke's copy of *Mittelreich* shows to what degree all those implicated in theatre—whether actors, performers, spectators, or critics—are always perceived as representatives of a larger community, distinguished by skin color, gender, physicality, social class, profession … . Thus, the questions that are currently dogging all democracies (who is represented in what way, by whom and with what right?) are reflected in the theatre. Can a bourgeois actress represent a refugee? Can the West represent the Global South? Can a man represent a woman? Is the representation of stereotypes and clichés (ethnic, gender, sexuality, etc.) an act of exposure or simply the repetition of degrading insults?

Recent discussions around blackface, the use of terms perceived as defamatory, and the like, call into question far more than just the right and the ability of white actors to portray characters of color. These are politically and artistically complex challenges that—like postcolonial discourse as a whole—have arrived late to continental European theatres.

The strategy of appropriation, which Recke negotiates with *Mittelreich*, has another complex aspect. When pop singer Miley Cyrus, who has a sharp instinct for using scandal as a marketing tool, twerked at the Video Music Awards a few years ago, a fierce and polemic discussion ensued. Was this a white woman stealing a piece of African American cultural identity for the purposes of her next hit? Was her appropriation of the move, marked by rhythmic and sexually explicit thrusting and shaking of the buttocks, an homage or a caricature? (Similar discussions accompanied Madonna's song "Vogue" more than 20 years earlier.) This, too, is a question of power relations: appropriation from "below" of what's "above" is self-empowerment, integration, assimilation, expansion of identity, or loss of identity. Appropriation in the opposite direction, robbery? A desire to understand? Recognition?

In their performance *Situation with Doppelgänger* (2015), theatremakers Julian Warner and Oliver Zahn trace the appropriation and marketing of Black and other minority dance forms in pop back to the time of minstrel shows of the nineteenth century, in which non-Black performers in makeup portrayed stereotypes—sometimes romanticized, sometimes hateful—of Black people. Later, Black dancers and musicians themselves were hired to perform in these shows, a feedback loop of clichés.

The questions raised by such cultural appropriations have not changed since: who owns such dances, who is allowed to dance them? When is imitation a subversive tactic, when does it reinforce existing power structures? In *Situation with Doppelgängers*, Warner and Zahn—one Black, the other white, but neither a trained dancer—synchronously interpret very differently connoted minstrel, pop, and folk dances, in which not only white performers imitate Black people, but Black dancers too, in a form of self-empowerment, imitate their white colonial "masters." Skating on thin ice, the two investigate—analytically and playfully at the same time—models of authenticity, identity, and sovereignty of interpretation.

Representation

The fact that such constructions have to be constantly renegotiated unmistakably shapes the performances created by the German-Ivorian group Gintersdorfer/Klaßen, not only thematically and aesthetically, but above all, in the way the group collaborates. If "the dancers sing, the comedians dance, the singers speak," then for Gintersdorfer/Klaßen this is a conscious speculation

> ... on unknown skills ... by which we avoid the pitfalls of representation in order to enter the realm of direct communication. The latter unfolds on every level and incorporates the audience, who are invited to mentally engage and maybe comment verbally. There's no such concept here, of unwelcome unforeseen disruption, we pursue a discursive dramaturgy without a regulated and timed progression. Untimed does not mean badly timed or long winded, it rather means timed by how things relate to the moment.[14]

The title of their performance *Black Thoughts Now — Chefferie* (2013) refers to a political-administrative model of the gathering of many equal leaders, which dates to precolonial times and is still practiced in sub-Saharan Africa parallel to official state structures. Thus "chefferie" is also a metaphor for German director Monika Gintersdorfer's own collaboration with powerful performers from the Ivory Coast, Germany, and, in this case, Rwanda and Congo. Although Gintersdorfer herself never appears onstage during the performance, contradictions and discursive or personal differences from the rehearsal process remain visible to the audience. Controversial interpretations and representations of African self-understanding are played off against each other with wit and irreverence, and every Western attempt to homogenize the image of the continent is undermined with humor. The performers do not avoid verbal or physical confrontation, nor do they shy away from politically sensitive stereotypes of national identities: the unease of the predominantly white audience is exactly what they want.

Julian Warner & Oliver Zahn: *Situation with Doppelgängers*

Representation

In *Chefferie* and many other Gintersdorfer/Klaßen pieces, the actor Hauke Heumann represents the white Westerners in the audience on stage, but at the same time quickly translates the text of the other performers back and forth between French, German, and English, allowing himself his own very personal commentary—a futile, but always hopeful and extremely funny struggle with a role that sits between self-denial and self-assertion.

Crises of Representation

In the Middle Ages, the matter was still relatively clear. The king has two bodies: a natural, human, mortal one, and a symbolic, collective-religious one that lasts forever.[15] The King is dead, long live the King! Later, in absolutism, there was only one body, the monarch was identical with the state—"L'état c'est moi" ("I am the state")—and no longer needed a deity for his legitimation. It became more complicated when the revolutions in North America and France suddenly granted sovereignty to the people. If power is distributed among everybody, no one person can embody it: the locus of power must remain empty.[16] Not only do political rulers no longer have any power of their own, the proxy power that they exercise over time belongs to an increasingly heterogeneous people. An impossible task: to represent something that cannot be represented. Thus, democracy is never complete; it always remains "to come," as philosopher Jacques Derrida puts it.[17]

It is inevitable, therefore, that modernity is threaded through with crises of representation—in politics, but also in art. First, painting and sculpture no longer wanted to be reduced to the task of mere illustration; then Marcel Duchamp brought the everyday into the museum with the ready-made, objects which at first seemed to represent nothing but themselves. Since the 1960s, performance art and Happenings have tried to escape representation by focusing entirely on presence, on the nowness of the situation that they themselves created. And institutional critique focused on the structural, organizational, and economic conditions of representation.

In the theatre, too, the fight against traditional notions of representation raged, with Antonin Artaud and Bertolt Brecht as the most prominent protagonists on opposing sides. While the former fought to eliminate the difference between representation and the represented and to fuse art and life into one, the latter wanted to transform them, make them transparent, and at the same time include those who were not sufficiently represented both artistically *and* politically. It becomes clear that Brecht's concept of *Gestus* (that is, a kind of referential pointing) is not only an aesthetic one: just as in democracy power is no longer embodied but becomes a gesture that refers to what is actually sovereign,[18] so it should always be clear that the actor's representation of a character is purely symbolic. *Gestus* is a finger that points to the impossibility of representation as well as the impossibility of non-representation, in both democracy and in the theatre. The two meanings of the word representation—that of portrayal and that of delegation—cannot be separated.

Regietheater and Early Postdramatic Theatre

It is the progressive theatre of the 1970s and 1980s that many in Europe and the USA consider to be almost synonymous with political art in general. And indeed at that time theatre was an undeniably relevant factor in many social debates (albeit in very different ways in West and East). At a time when opposing ideologies were still powerful and the separation between the blocs clearly marked, the theatre engaged in a multitude of political concerns by representing the misery of the world—from the Vietnam War to apartheid

Representation

in South Africa to the everyday adversities of a local working-class family. While in the East the subversive force often lay in hidden or coded messages, in the West open provocations and spectators loudly leaving the auditorium in protest were an important part of the repertoire. Whether using newly written dramatic texts or ever-modernized classics: radical interpretations were an essential feature of a *Regietheater* (director's theatre) that, despite its many new approaches, on the whole remained trapped in mimesis no matter how abstract it might have been. Even if the political theatre of the time often succeeded in generating an awareness of the systemic reasons undergirding the abuses it depicted, it was largely unable to escape the dilemma that its representations were merely symbolic repetitions of precisely those evils which it actually wanted to combat. Brecht had already given this phenomenon a name in the early 1930s, referring to it as "cannibal drama": "The physical exploitation of the poor was followed by psychological exploitation. Double ministerial salaries were thrown at those mimes who could imitate the torments of the exploited as faithfully as possible... ."[19] The object of pity generates feelings of grief, affliction, guilt, or even anger among the spectators, who in all likelihood—at least structurally—are implicated in keeping this very system of exploitation alive.

> The two meanings of the word representation—that of portrayal and that of delegation—cannot be separated.

Ultimately, the theatre often simply continues what Brecht analyzed in his *Short Organum for the Theatre*: "The theatre as we know it shows the structure of society (represented on the stage) as incapable of being influenced by society (in the auditorium)."[20] Not only the play on stage, but the entire theatrical setup, not to mention the hierarchies in the institution itself, all reproduce the system they aim to criticize. In the words of theatremaker René Pollesch:

> [Actresses must] reproduce on stage the sexism that reigns in society …, legitimized by the dramatic canon, which knows no female characters, where in *Robbers* Amalie briefly pops up, wearing even in today's productions a skimpy dress to provide for a bit of eroticism, and then goes out again, and has nothing to say … .[21]

In clear opposition to this representational practice, primarily from the 1990s onwards, a theatre began to emerge which did not just want to reform dominant models but revolutionize them outside the established structures. Postdramatic theatre, devised theatre, live art, performance theatre, independent theatre—there are many labels for this genre, which is usually not easy to define due to the variety of its forms and its overlaps with other artistic disciplines. Even more than skepticism about the dominant role of the text, to which productions in dramatic theatre are almost always subordinated, criticism of the use of mimetic representation was at the core of these new aesthetics and working methods. Author-directors like John Jesurun and René Pollesch and collectives like Gob Squad and She She Pop refused as presumptuous to talk about others, their problems, guilt, and suffering. Instead, they turned their gaze to themselves, to their pop-cultural environment and the theatre as a medium. In this they aligned with what Douglas Coupland writes in his then much-quoted novel *Generation X*: "Either our lives become stories, or there's just no way to get through them."[22]

Not only the play on stage, but the entire theatrical setup, not to mention the hierarchies in the institution itself, all merely reproduce the system they aim to criticize.

They made the place of theatre visible as meeting point, but also as machinery, while—unapologetically subjective—negotiating on stage their own small environment: a globalized, urban, creative, semiprecarious middle class, which was still in the making and therefore had to continuously define itself. However, the very po-

Gintersdorfer/Klaßen: *Chefferie*

litical impulse to let reflection begin at home carries the danger of confusing one's own living room with the world, as British-German group Gob Squad self-critically summed it up years later in *Western Society* (2013). Here, too, as usual, the life of the artists' own bubble is brought to the stage, but the title provides the framework for an ironic-nostalgic look thrown at a white Western society that has long ceased to exist—that perhaps never existed. As if seen through the wrong end of a telescope, that which is very close suddenly appears very far away.

Since the 2000s, a number of theatremakers have taken a different approach to dealing with dramatic theatre's representational trap, increasingly turning to documentary formats and opening the stage for the self-portrayal of "real people." Directors' collectives such as Rimini Protokoll, the Manchester-based company Quarantine, or the Argentinian author and director Lola Arias have developed in their work with "experts of the everyday" (Rimini Protokoll) very specific and very different dramaturgies of care which often succeed in meeting both the needs of the performers and the artistic demands of the performance. It is essential for the worldwide success of such a "documentary theatre" that it neither limits itself to the ultimately finite reserve of existing or newly created dramatic figures, nor to a theatre of peers on which most other independent theatremakers exclusively lean. That it introduces people one rarely, or never, sees in this way. That it does not show them—like on reality TV and talk shows—in real or artificial states of emergency, but in ones where they radiate calm and self-confidence. And that it makes no secret of the fact that in this staged authenticity, the performers also just play a role, albeit the role of their lives.

Such games of (self-)representation have been further intensified by groups like Switzerland's Theater HORA which is—alongside groups such as the Australian Back to Back Theatre, the French ensembles Création Ephémère and Oiseau-Mouche, the Belgian Theater Stap, the Polish Teatr 21 and the Dutch group Maatwerk—one of the best-known and oldest companies working with cognitively impaired actors, in this case mostly affected by Down syndrome. It counters the usual image of society with one in which those who are considered "not normal"—who are usually invisible, who are considered unproductive, uncultured, perhaps even uncanny—take up space. The power of this counter-image lies precisely in the fact that it remains fragile and fragmented. The strong, often unpredictable personalities of the performers infiltrate otherwise too-obvious statements with constant ambiguity.

As a guest director, French choreographer Jérôme Bel made his own precarious position clear in *Disabled Theater* (2012) by having his strict stage directions unmistakably announced on stage during the performance, emphasizing the implicit hierarchy of the production. At the same time, however, the performers carried out the tasks in whatever way suited them (which was sometimes not at all). Bel, whose reputation is itself based on breaking the rules, found the extent to which the dominant conventions of the theatre were constantly disregarded confusing and impressive:

> When I started to work with them, I was nearly fainting. And then suddenly, I understood that there were still a lot of those theatre rules that I didn't question myself. Like being noisy backstage. At first, I was starting to jump on stage and yell at them. But then I realised that this little incident revealed only my own rules. I still have a lot of work to do.[23]

Addiction to control meets subversion, conceptual art meets camp. Christoph Schlingensief explained in the context of his *Freakstars 3000* (2002), a TV talent show with mentally and physically disabled participants, many of whom, such as Werner Brecht, Mario Garzaner, Helga Stöwhase, and Achim von Paczensky, had already been seen in his films or theatre works: "The freak is the situation itself that forces us to distinguish what is normal and what is not."²⁴

Visibly inspired by poststructuralist theories, all such approaches rebel in very different ways against the hegemony of the text with a new complexity of theatrical signs: if the text no longer necessarily has the first and last word, it is possible for anything to come to the fore: movement, space, sound, light, the presence of the performers, the audience... .

Instead of (artificially) representing a situation—that is, showing another reality in order to criticize it—the aim is to create one's own (real) situation in the co-presence of the audience, as theatre scholar Hans-Thies Lehmann writes in *Postdramatic Theatre*: "In contrast to other arts, which produce an object and/or are communicated through media, here [in theatre] the aesthetic act itself (the performing) as well as the act of reception (the theatre going) take place as a real doing in the here and now... . The emission and reception of signs and signals take place simultaneously."²⁵

> Inspired by poststructuralist theories, all such approaches rebel in very different ways against the hegemony of the text with a new complexity of theatrical signs.

The focus on the medium and form of theatre itself, the distrust of closed narratives and psychological causality, the desire to enable individual experiences in which all spectators must find their own routes to interpretation, also had an impact on the concept of the political in theatre. This was now sought above all in the "how" of its representation, no longer in the "what" of its concrete political content. Philosophers like Jacques Rancière offered a broad theoretical basis for rethinking the medium of theatre through the analysis of the "aesthetic regime" and the role of the viewer as an "emancipated spectator."²⁶

Theater HORA/Jérôme Bel: *Disabled Theater*

Postdramatic theatre and conceptual dance consistently responded to the often simplistic or moralizing use of terms such as truth, reality, and politics with a complex interplay of layers, ambiguities, and challenges. In this way, they have opened up new perspectives and artistic possibilities, which ultimately also strongly influenced the field of dramatic theatre.

Taking viewers, all with their own experiences, seriously as co-authors in this way was an important impulse. But it had a significant side effect: the audience was seen less as a possible collective than as a gathering of individuals. Postdramatic theatre and conceptual dance—once again corresponding to broader changes in society—created viewers who may have emancipated themselves from the director's imposed imagination, but also more closely resembled the ideal neoliberal subject, which seeks its individuality above all in active consumption.

Politics and the Political

In discussions about political theatre in recent years, reference is usually made to the distinction between *politics* and *the political*. This differentiation is not new, but it has gained in importance, especially since the end of supposed certainties after the fall of the Berlin Wall. Above all, French philosophers such as Jean-Luc Nancy, Alain Badiou, Jacques Rancière, and Claude Lefort (but also others like Giorgio Agamben, Ernesto Laclau, and Chantal Mouffe) have answered the crumbling of ideological foundations in East and West with (as the political scientist Oliver Marchart writes) "post-fundamentalist" theories, in which *the political* plays a central role.

Politics here includes, with slightly different boundaries according to different approaches, the concrete field of state functions and state action (parties, government, etc.). It is the quotidian politics of politicians and parliamentary routines. The problem: in the end, it always remains pragmatic, at best a vigorous, slow drilling of hard boards, but leaving hardly any room for utopias, for the big questions. This is why *politics* usually does not have a good reputation among political theorists.

The political, on the other hand, is harder to define. In its common use, it gestures somewhat vaguely to the dimension of the social, sometimes of the collective, to the sphere in which political movements manifest from Occupy Wall Street to the yellow vests in France. *The political* thus denotes the nonpragmatic, the unfiltered, the direct: "To refer to the political and not to politics … is to speak of everything that constitutes a polity beyond direct partisan competition for the exercise of power, day-to-day government action, and the ordinary life of institutions," writes political scientist Pierre Rosanvallon.[27]

More fundamental is the use of the term in the thinking of the above-mentioned postfundamentalist theorists—whereby the word "fundamental" obviously points at a paradox. For in fact, *the political* constitutes something like the foundation of a philosophy in which there are no longer any reliable foundations: *the political* is the ever-changing, uncertain, contingent base of *politics*. It is that which always questions politics—and only in this way makes a vibrant democracy possible. Without order (and thus a foundation) society cannot exist. But this order is not final; it must be constantly renegotiated. Its truths are working theses, to which Derrida's aforementioned concept of a democracy "to come" also refers.[28]

This distinction between politics and the political is important and helpful. It exposes the inner contradictions of political action—and shows that democracy must be constantly re-won, re-founded. By opening up the possibility of political imagination, of alternative thinking and acting, it not only enables an understanding of the numerous extra-parliamentary movements across the world, but also of the special potential of art as a political space.

But the focus on the political also carries the risk of pure "philosophism," as Marchart calls it: "The belief in a 'pure' political then becomes the intellectual variant of a destructive disenchantment with politics, instead of encouraging productive action." Marchart himself notes elsewhere that this can also be applied to culture: "Incidentally, a comparable operation can be found in arts discourse when it is claimed that all art is inherently political, in order to ultimately aim at nothing other than the delegitimization of actually political art."²⁹

In fact, a generation of philosophers who had derived their theories directly from their own political experiences and commitments—Michel Foucault fought with the *Groupe d'information sur les prisons* for human rights in prisons, Alain Badiou was involved in migration and asylum policy with the *Organisation politique*, Jacques Rancière was briefly a member of a Maoist group, to name just a few—has been gradually replaced by philosophers (and artists, dramaturges, curators, etc.) who built on these considerations and further abstracted them—but all too often without tying them back into their own present, concrete reality.

> A second-hand, homeopathic understanding of political philosophy and art has become the basis of many contemporary cultural discourses.

And so it is not just the theatre world that has become accustomed to calling philosophical theories and works of art political even if they are merely based on ideas that were themselves already abstracted from the concrete political impulses that ignited them. A second-hand, homeopathic understanding of political philosophy and art has become the basis of many contemporary cultural discourses.

In the process, the constant awareness of the complexity of concepts such as truth, reality, and even politics often maneuvers us into a dead end. Our understanding and description of the world is either too simplistic or too complex, too populist or too hermetic. Either we include too much or we exclude too many. We have reached a point where the necessary awareness that everything is contingent often has become an excuse for intellectual relativism.

Jacques Rancière's writings, in particular, have been used for this purpose since the late 1990s. His skepticism towards every clear political statement in art and his strong confidence in the power of its "indetermination"[30] helped to pave the way for very broad definitions of the political. His thesis that art's resistance lies above all in that it creates "ruptures in the perceptual order, overturnings of sensible hierarchies"[31] frequently becomes a blank check for a form of art that (often only apparently) shakes up viewing habits, but otherwise does not reveal any political concern.

Therefore Hans-Thies Lehmann's dictum that "the political, the political effect, the political substance [of the theatre]" should be sought "in the *how* of the presentation"[32] is varied and supplemented by current politically engaged theatremakers for whom theatre's political substance lies precisely in reconciling the what and the how of representation. As great as the political potential of an aesthetic of confusion and altered perceptions may be, it cannot replace the examination of a concrete object. Knowing that the dilemma of representation is never a purely formal one, theatremakers in recent times have increasingly tried to maintain a self-reflexive awareness of questions of form and, at the same time, to put it to work for concrete political content—thus artistically combining complexity and clarity in the interplay of aesthetics and ethics.

Anthropocene, Animism, and Posthumanism

But the question of who or what is actually represented has even more far-reaching implications. In recent years, the idea that we are living in a new age, the Anthropocene, has become prevalent: an era that, as the name suggests, is significantly shaped by humans and their deeds.

The fact that humanity has massively altered the planet may not sound surprising at first. However, the concept of the Anthropocene goes literally deeper; it is not cultural-historical, but geochronological. The traces of humanity can be detected not only on the surface; they belong to the geological, biological, and atmospheric processes of the Earth in the long term, or even forever.

This finding has raised the pressing demand for fundamentally different models of life in art as well, including variants of a new materialism and theories of trans- or posthumanism (which in various ways expel the human at least from the center of creation, reconfigure it, or even abolish it altogether).

Above all, the concept of animism (that is, the view that everything on earth has a soul or spirit, including animals, plants, stones, rivers…), originally stemming from nineteenth century ethnology, has become the starting point for numerous new considerations. In artistic discourse, a key example is the exhibition *Animism* at the Haus der Kulturen der Welt in Berlin (2012), which blurred the boundaries between life and nonlife and thus, as a critique of the either/or dualism of modernity, demanded a different view of "animated matter, animated or socialized nature, agential things, spirits, transformations"[33] and their representation.

One of the most prominent representatives of a fundamental criticism of modernism is—alongside biologist and feminist theorist Donna Haraway and philosopher Isabelle Stengers—the late French philosopher Bruno Latour, whose work calls for expanding the social to include non-human actors and dissolving the distinction between supposed opposites such as subject and object. The "Parliament of Things" he envisaged is intended to enable people, animals, plants, objects as actors and "actants" (as he calls non-human actors) to jointly determine for themselves *how* they make decisions in the first place and *how* they want to live together.[34]

To imagine this as a theatrical performance, albeit a utopian one, is probably not far off the mark. After all, the term "actor," a central concept in Latour's theory, comes, as he himself writes elsewhere, "from the stage." Using it "means that it's never clear who and what is acting when we act since an actor on stage is never alone in acting."³⁵ In this context one might think of the Polish theatre visionary Tadeusz Kantor, who in legendary works such as *The Dead Class* (1975) understood dolls, objects, and actors as equal performers. People and things merge into "organic objects."

And so the examination of representation in the theatre, when carried out to its logical ends, also includes nonhuman entities, for example when Mette Ingvartsen choreographs imaginary landscapes of fog and light in *evaporated landscapes* (2009); when Jozef Wouters expands the Natural History Museum in Brussels with a *Zoological Institute for Recently Extinct Species* (2013); and when David Weber-Krebs, in his long-term project *Balthazar* (since 2011), directs a donkey as a rather stubborn performer on stage and thus puts the other actors in the situation of always having to anticipate how the animal will react, act, and understand the space.³⁶

Above all, such work raises questions, and ones which are usually not high on political agendas. Like those that became the starting point for the playful project for young audiences *Animals of Manchester (including HUMANZ)* (2019) by Hamburg theatremaker Sibylle Peters: "What if animals had equal rights, had civic rights, what if we humanz had the right to claim our animalship, be animals together, no species better or worse than the other?"³⁷ Influenced by Donna Haraway among others,³⁸ the three-day project drew up the vision of a city in which "all kinds of animals, including humans,"* tested out together what peace between the species might look like:

---

*   The pragmatic, real political question of the ecological sustainability of artistic activities also belongs here. With its Burning Ice Festival (2009–2016), the Kaaitheater in Brussels in particular has presented a wide range

Representation

> A heterotopian zone complete with an edible shopping centre for squirrels and birds, a townhall with a standing conference of animals including the mayor, a retired milk cow, pigeons and microbes, a cemetery to remember extinct species, a university for dogs and other pets to teach humanz, a beetles' film institute and a life art library.[39]

Trembling Androids, Sweating Avatars

But a potted plant on stage does not yet make a Parliament of Things nor do rabbits as protagonists alone establish a space of posthumanism. New materialism, object-oriented ontology, animism, artificial intelligence, artificial bodies, virtual worlds, algorithms everywhere—the somewhat old-fashioned, analogue, anthropocentric medium of theatre finds it more difficult than, for example, the visual arts to deal with developments that want to banish humans from the center of thinking and feeling. The perspective of the theatre does not come *from* the future, but rather is directed *toward* the future. Theatre cannot stage or represent a world in which humanity has dissolved into nature, technology, or data. But it can reflect the rapid changes and explore spaces for action from a human point of view.

Stefan Kaegi's solo for an android, *Uncanny Valley* (2018), sums it up: While Rimini Protokoll has always refused to have their protagonists portrayed by actors, in this work the human is replaced

---

of artistic discussions on such questions and has intensively involved its institutional work processes in them, as well. One of the most consistent artists in this realm is choreographer Tino Sehgal, who has not boarded an airplane for more than twenty years and often also forbids performers from flying in connection with his works. Recently, the choreographer Jérôme Bel has committed himself to a similar attitude: instead of sending performers around the world, he develops local versions of his works and increasingly holds rehearsals for them via Skype.

Sibylle Peters: *Animals of Manchester (including HUMANZ)*

by a robot that is the spitting image of the writer Thomas Melle, whose story is being told. On the one hand, this mechanical doll resembles Melle more closely than any actor probably ever could; on the other hand, he is more foreign to him, his artificiality an indissoluble alienation effect.

Indeed, in the course of the evening it becomes less and less clear who is actually representing whom. For as much as the monologue is about the double being superior to the original—no phobias, no diseases, no mortality—the human still holds the strings, and wields this power with relish: turning off the apparatus, setting tasks it cannot accomplish, and above all, putting every word in its mouth. In the end, the android is nothing but a fancy dictation machine, and yet a deeply uncanny one: because of its likeness and because of its unlikeness to humans at the same time. Androids, doppelgängers, and mannequins are disturbing because we relate to them.* Because not only are robots becoming more and more like us, we are becoming more and more like robots as well; cyborgs in many respects already now.⁴²

> But a potted plant on stage does not yet make a Parliament of Things nor do rabbits as protagonists alone establish a space of posthumanism.

Susanne Kennedy stages a similar game under reverse auspices in *Coming Society* (2019), in which avatars are inadequately portrayed by humans. Their trembling, their quick breathing, their

---

* The Japanese roboticist Masahiro Mori coined the term "uncanny valley." This refers to the graphical curve that describes human acceptance of androids: at first, as similarity to humans increases, they also appear more familiar—but from a certain humanlike degree onwards, the familiarity suddenly collapses. Only when the robot can no longer be distinguished from humans at all does it rise again. So perhaps it is no coincidence that the android Data from the series *Star Trek: The Next Generation* (1987–1994) loves to perform in theatre. For him, the medium is the ultimate hurdle to being human.

sweating are the ties that bind them to the audience. Just as it is impossible for the Melle-bot to dance, it is impossible for Kennedy's performers to disembody themselves in a way that would be appropriate for virtual beings.

While robots may not lack perfection much longer, the very human flaw of defectiveness will continue to belong to the theatre, which has always been a medium of radical presence and of the human, that is, of compromise and failure. Even if theatre has been trying for centuries to produce performances that can be repeated with as much accuracy as possible night after night, its essential quality lies in never achieving precisely that. Every trembling hand, every flubbed line, every accident, every interruption, but also every swallow, every deep breath refers directly to the shared present, to the time spent together by the artists and spectators. And this reaches far beyond the theatre space. A mistake in the system creates more awareness of the fragility of all life than the most perfect dramaturgy. Heiner Müller's statement that "what is particular to the theatre … is not the presence of the living spectator, but of the potentially dying one"[40] finds a contemporary continuation in the remark of the Japanese robot scientist Hiroshi Ishiguro, that our mortality is the real reason we find robots uncanny: "They do not age, in theory they can live forever."[41]

Protest against Brett Bailey's *Exhibit B* in London

IDENTITY POLITICS

Petitions, demonstrations, boycotts, large-scale police operations, even helicopters: in the end, the showings of Brett Bailey's *Exhibit B* (2012), which explicitly references ethnological shows popular in the nineteenth and early twentieth centuries, were cancelled by the Barbican Centre in London in September 2014.[42] While the performance installation had previously been presented without any major fuss in Austria, Germany, and even elsewhere in Great Britain, from now on it was met by serious controversies at the subsequently planned stops. By critiquing the logic of representation these conflicts appealed against the repetition of violence through its depiction and questioned whether *Exhibit B* was anything other than exoticization and voyeurism in a shiny new package. But underneath all this a more fundamental unease in society was brought to light. Bailey's show, in which Black bodies, not exactly shown with sensitivity, are displayed on pedestals or behind wire mesh, had become a catalyst for a larger social debate about racist clichés and unaddressed colonial legacies. The protestors' slogan "No more human zoo!" took aim at more than just this specific restaging of a historical display by a white South African director.*

---

*   Around the same time, Dutch artist Dries Verhoeven was pursuing a similar concept with *Ceci n'est pas...* (2013); a key difference is that this work's display cases were placed in public urban space (e.g., in Utrecht, Oslo, Helsinki, Montreal, and Hamburg) in order to provoke unplanned encounters. Over the course of ten days, a rotating cast of people were

Identity Politics

While the accusations levelled against Bailey were addressing the fact that he was reproducing, regardless of critical intent, in an ambiguous way, images that were clearly discriminatory, the accusations against US-American artist Dana Schutz turned the screw still further in their criticism of representation. Exhibited at the 2017 Whitney Biennial, Schutz's painting *Open Casket* leaves no doubt about the artist's stance: it is a clear indictment of the perpetrators. It depicts Emmett Till, a fourteen-year-old Black boy murdered by two white men in the United States in 1955, lying in an open coffin. The photograph on which the image is based has been an important symbol for the civil rights struggle in the US-American South. It was a photo that Till's mother explicitly wanted to show the world: This is what these people did to my son![43]

> **Pressure built up over decades or centuries does not always release with precision or in controlled doses.**

Dana Schutz's appropriation of this motif quickly gave rise to protests from Black artists insisting that a white artist does not have the right to use this image, benefiting from it symbolically and perhaps financially. In an open letter, artist Hannah Black even demanded that the work be not only removed from the exhibition, but destroyed.[44]

Broken-off discussions, quickly escalating Facebook comments, the occasional cancelled performance or lecture: while not all such incidents make the headlines, they are nonetheless symptoms of an increasingly hostile discursive climate in art and theatre, cre-

---

exhibited, all of whom touched on social taboos, including a transsexual, a prostitute with dwarfism, a naked old woman, a praying Muslim, a Black man in a loincloth and with a chain around his ankle, and a nearly naked man with a nearly naked little girl on his lap. This work, too, provoked numerous protests.

Identity Politics

ating quite a degree of uncertainty.* Given the context of Black Lives Matter, #metoo, and other analog and virtual movements, the vehemence with which everyday discrimination, harassment, and physical, psychological, and symbolic violence are discussed is not especially surprising. Pressure built up over decades or centuries does not always release with precision or in controlled doses. The belief that all secondary contradictions such as racism, lack of equal rights for women, or pollution and resource extraction would dissolve on their own once the primary contradiction (that is, between labor and capital) is removed has been a pillar of leftist folklore for far too long.

Infiltrated Terms and Special Interests

Such questions about the representation of marginalized communities and the underprivileged are undergirded by concepts and political agendas which, despite their differences, have been grouped

---

* It should, however, not be forgotten that artistic censorship usually (and much more effectively) comes from the other side, often buoyed by claims of harm to a religious group. Art exhibitions in Moscow shut down by the state (e.g., *Caution! Religion* (2003) and *Forbidden Art* (2006)) are part of the picture, as are demonstrations and boycotts of productions such as *Golgata Picnic* (2011) by Argentine director Rodrigo García in France and Poland, which was removed from the program of the Malta Festival in 2014 for fear of attacks. Romeo Castellucci's *On the Concept of the Face, Regarding the Son of God* (2010), a production drenched in pathos and suffering, was greeted by numerous demonstrations and interrupted performances, especially in France. In 2013, a production by Croatian director Oliver Frljić did not even make it as far as the premiere at a theatre in Krakow. In 2017 his interpretation of Stanisław Wyspiański's *Klątwa* (The Curse) at Teatr Powszechny in the Polish capital Warsaw triggered a series of heated protests in front of the theatre.

together under the term *identity politics*. Identity politics refers to a model, ultimately based more in practice than theory, which was originally developed in the 1970s by women of color in the USA as a critique of a class struggle dominated by men and of a feminism that was overwhelmingly white, Western, and not least heterosexual. As the Combahee River Collective, a Black feminist lesbian socialist organization active in Boston, writes in 1977, "We believe that the most profound and potentially most radical politics come directly out of our own identity,"[45] because this identity is, due to overlapping oppressions, different in significant ways from that of Black heterosexual or white lesbian women, for example. A decade later, lawyer and civil rights advocate Kimberlé Crenshaw coined the originally legal term *intersectionality*, to point to the fact that this confluence of different experiences of discrimination—due to race, class, gender, or other characteristics—was in fact something more than just the sum of the various oppressions.[46]

Discrimination does not only come in forms that are large-scale, unambiguous, obviously violent, degrading, insulting, or mentally or physically harmful. Perhaps even more effective, because happening all the time and more difficult to name, are the countless microaggressions that shape the everyday life of many: small assaults, often made unconsciously or even with good intentions. Even that which is not meant to cause pain can be painful—like the notorious question "Where are you really from?" posed time and again to people whose skin color marks them as "other." In many cases, microaggressions—both real and perceived—add up to ongoing and fundamental experiences of discrimination.

Identity politics is therefore both an analytical tool and a weapon wielded by oppressed groups in the struggle for their specific interests—a somewhat paradoxical reaction to the fact that the very definition of this group is often created precisely by the discrimination they experience, by the box (Black, female, gay, etc.) into which each is shoved. It is an attempt to use a negative classification for

Oliver Frljić: *Klątwa (The Curse)*

positive ends and to put it to use for powerful advocacy, but also to reclaim pride and dignity. Postcolonial theorist Gayatri Chakravorty Spivak described this conscious "use of positivist essentialism in a scrupulously visible political interest"[47] as *strategic essentialism*.

Calling it strategic is appropriate because while there are pragmatic benefits to such an approach, it is accompanied by fundamental theoretical problems. Identity politics is after all a double-edged sword: the tactical means of emphasizing shared identities in order to put the common before the divisive also plays into the hands of a more or less closed concept of identity. Strategic as this essentialism (a concept suggesting that individuals or groups possess an essence, a true core, a sort of natural identity) may be, it still stands in contradiction to the idea of identity as a cultural, performative construction that arises only in interaction with one's environment—as a mix of narratives, out of the overlapping of stories that we tell ourselves and that others tell about us. Another hazard of strategic essentialism, which has become quite influential in the fight for civil rights and for feminist struggle as well, lies in its attractiveness to right-wing ideologues propagating the right to preserve what they assume to be *their* national or racial essence. Spivak herself problematized the term on a number of occasions.[48]

Indeed, the far right has long since discovered the concept of identity politics, and pilfered whatever seemed useful, not flinching about theoretical details. The Identitarian movement, which is widespread in Europe, North America, and Australia and has roots in the French youth movement *génération identitaire*, fights side by side with the alt-right movement in the United States to protect its own white, Western, and primarily male identity against alleged external threats. At its most extreme the paranoia manufactures apocalyptic images of a "white genocide" enacted by pretty much everyone (but especially Muslims) who is not white.[49] Slightly more diplomatic versions settle for turning leftist demands regarding diversity inside out, by insisting that their own (white) cultures have the right to their identities and that this right is under attack, as expressed for example in the platform of the German right wing party AfD: "Against [the ideology of multiculturalism] the state and civil society must with confidence defend German cultural identity as the dominant culture."[50] Cameroonian philosopher Achille Mbembe states:

> Identity politics was once a means of emancipation, for example in the feminist movement, and a means of inclusion by which more people could be united. Today it is being instrumentalized for the opposite: exclusion. The potential losers within society are mobilized against those on the outside. And the usual rallying cries, such as religion and race, are used to do it. Identity politics has thus become a threat to democracy. Anyone who wants to destroy liberal democracy must invest in identity politics. Still, the crucial question of our time is what connects us with others who are not "us". Because, in reality, the same problems affect us all.[51]

Strategies used in identity politics increasingly came under fire after Donald Trump was elected President of the United States, when the accusation arose from the left as well as the right that, actually, liberal metropolitan elites and left-wing activists were the ones who made Trump, Brexit, and the like possible in the first place—thanks to allegedly mixed-up priorities, which included focusing too strongly on so-called special interests and, above all, failing to connect with the left's actual base (the working class). US-American political scientist Mark Lilla set the tone when, shortly after Trump's election, he put the left-wing concept of diversity in opposition to a conservative concept of national unity, concluding it would be better to emphasize the commonalities of the American people than their differences.[52] While it has its own irony when conservative liberals like Lilla or historian Francis Fukuyama, author of *The End of History*, blame Trump's election conveniently on their own political opponents, leftists too (like Slovenian philosopher

Slavoj Žižek) have pointed to identity politics as the main culprit for the electoral defeats of the progressive camp.[53] There is much that can be said in response: for example, that the left's years of flirtation with neoliberalism are perhaps more to blame for the alienation of their own base than the demand for equal rights for all. Even if the worldwide success the right has recently enjoyed among Western working and lower middle classes cuts the progressive left to the quick, the way to win them back can hardly be to pit different precarious groups against one another, as French sociologist Didier Eribon makes clear:

> [One must] not oppose social questions, that is to say the working class and the problems of the lower class in general, to the questions of feminism, rights for the marginalized, or protection of the environment ... Because everything is interconnected in many different ways... . At certain times, certain political goals are in the foreground. But that doesn't mean that all other political struggles are suddenly unimportant or illegitimate. All areas of conflict are related, they overlap, but they do not supersede one another.[54]

And so it remains a balancing act: recognizing, respecting, and struggling against a wide variety of discriminations, while simultaneously bridging divisions in a time when broader alliances of progressive groups are urgently needed to counter the increasing threat from the right. Even if sometimes fundamentalist forms of identity politics, or appropriations of the term "trigger" from trauma therapy for personal uses, obscure the view of the real political situation because they exhaust themselves in the symbolic or the private, the demand for justice and solidarity is not a particular interest.

A theatre that understands itself as political must be aware of its effects—and of its side effects. First of all this means, quite simply, working not to exclude, discriminate against, or insult anyone, and not to belittle the suffering of others through certain forms of representation.

What might sound banal, however, gets to the heart of the matter. Acknowledging one's own implication in deeply rooted racist or sexist structures can be painful and unsettle one's self-image in many ways. The process begins with apparently innocent childhood experiences—which stories, which costumes, which games did we love?—and continues, but does not end with questions of which traditions, cultural and artistic experiences, and rituals we wouldn't want to let go of as adults. Trying to undo that which, for example, has been shaped and normalized by the white male heterosexual gaze is no speedy process; instead, it is laborious, sometimes annoying, sometimes painful. Because while the rallying cry "Check your privilege!" seemingly points at individuals, it primarily references underlying organizational, aesthetic, and historical systems.* Dealing with such deeply anchored structures, metaphors, and narratives is difficult; it demands the constant (re)negotiation of what can and cannot be said or done and which opinions have to be endured even if you don't like them.

> **A theatre that understands itself as political must be aware of its effects—and of its side effects.**

This has less to do with targeting specific works of art (and specific artists), which in some cases might be more justified than in others, than it does with the struggle against cultural hegemony. First we have to change perspectives, and then structures. As permanently as possible.

---

* At the 2005 Venice Biennale, the legendary US-American action art collective Guerrilla Girls used a poster campaign to make the point that the number of paintings by women languishing in the basements of major museums is by no means small: "Where are the women artists of Venice? Underneath the men."

Privileges and Unproductive Silences

And so we find ourselves in the midst of seemingly never-ending conflicts: about expressions that were not intended to insult but that hurt just the same, about lack of representation, about images that should no longer be shown, about who's talking too much and who's saying too little. It is a political strategy hinging on the assumption that there is only a small window of public attention. A brief period in which paradigms must be so completely shifted that the anticipated pushback won't be able to reverse things again to the way they were before. The target might be sometimes overshot; headwinds have already been factored in.

This approach is certainly effective, as one can see in the many debates in the field of theatre over artistic programming and the makeups of ensembles, as well as over forms of interaction and cooperation in the broader artistic environment. Yet there are downsides to a political approach that essentially shaves away at a problem, leaving even onlookers in a cloud of sawdust. To stay silent can be a political act if it gives unheard stories the chance to be heard. To just shut up out of cowardice or laziness, though, is far less productive—especially when it means that disagreement simply gets voiced even more vigorously behind closed doors.

When it comes to programming theatres and festivals, there is often a fine line between self-restraint and self-censorship. What gets left unsaid because there is a real reason to do so, and what only because the discussion would be too much work? Where silence is due not to understanding but to fear of sanctions or, on the opposite end of the spectrum, well-meaning pity, no actual political victory has been achieved. Emotional blackmailing stands in the way of independent, political, systemic thinking. If certain attitudes become self-evident and claiming victimhood purely a rhetorical trick, real understanding, acceptance, learning, and participation become much less likely.

This is all the more true given that some of the toughest battles are fought among those whose views are barely distinguishable from just a few paces away. For theatre and art with their insistence on utopian thinking, it is indeed especially necessary to put their own houses in order, knowing that they will be measured by their own standards. But taking up a fight within a bubble should not mean forgetting about the rest of the world, as Achille Mbembe reminds us:

> Striking in this regard is the apparent shift from a politics of reason to a politics of experience, if not of viscerality. In the eyes of many, personal experience has become the new way of being at home in the world. It's like the bubble that holds the foam at a distance. Experience nowadays trumps reason. We are led to believe that sensibility, emotions, affect, sentiments and feelings are the real stuff of subjecthood and therefore of radical agency. Paradoxically, in the paranoid tenor of our epoch, this is very much in tune with the dominant strictures of neoliberal individualism. It is also in line with the ongoing reconfigurations of the relation between technology, reason and other human faculties.
>
> Whatever the case, this has given rise to ambiguous forms of collective mobilisation, most of which we shouldn't romanticise. Behind the mask of radicalism, there is something fundamentally ambivalent in the political discourse of decolonisation when, for instance, the injunction to decolonise goes hand in hand with high tolerance for xenophobia or the desire to control and defend what amounts to inverse racial borders. There is something fundamentally debilitating when subaltern resistance politics is limited to an endless performance of purity and self-righteousness, or to a competition about who has suffered the most on the spiralling scale of victimization... .
>
> The political cannot be reduced to the painstaking management of emotionally safe spaces and shared atmospheres. Radical agency is not about the sharing of boundaries. It is about deborderisation. It is simply not true that unless I have undergone the exact same experience as the other, I know nothing about his or her pain and

should simply shut up. Insofar as to be human is to open oneself up to the possibility always already there of becoming (an)other, such a conception of self and identity is by definition antihuman. The political in our time must start from the imperative to reconstruct the world in common. For the idea of decolonisation to have any purchase at a planetary scale, it cannot start from the assumption that I am purer than my neighbour.[55]

Offended Offenders

On the other hand, there is quite a lot of self-pity, passive aggressively expressed in phrases like "I'm still allowed to say that, right?" despite the fact that currently everything that we are supposedly not allowed to say in fact gets said more often and more publicly than it has been in a long time. Alongside clear political concerns, there is above all a noticeable sentimentality, a profound sense of woundedness produced by the notion that the world is changing. The so-called center of society clamors for the supposed artistic right to offend others, at the same time insisting that these others have no reason to be offended: haven't, after all, white actors always performed in blackface; didn't the N-word once mean something completely different? Since it is clear that in art as well as in life insulting the powerful is considered more honorable than kicking those who are already down, everyone is at pains to paint themselves as the actual victim. It has its own irony that those who otherwise extol the poetic power of language are not seldom the quickest to dismiss, as pure chimeras from the politically-correct language police, the idea that terms, undertones, and metaphorical connotations could have any real societal impact.

"Words can be like tiny doses of arsenic: they are swallowed unnoticed, appear to have no effect, and then after a little time the toxic reaction sets in after all,"[56] wrote philologist Victor Klemperer about the language of Nazism. Right-wing parties today are once again changing the political discourse, not least by shifting what is said and how, and what may be said and how. Art forms that work with words and images must be particularly careful not to play into their hands through thoughtless speech. Language is performative. It does not simply reflect hegemonic relationships; it is not merely the stage on which they play. It creates and re-creates them, without end.

And, if we are to be honest, seldom has there been a cultural war with as little iconoclasm as this one. Just consider that some of the loudest voices now railing against the supposed terrorism of the virtuous flirted in their youth, Little Red Book in their fists, with a cultural revolution of a completely different brutality. The theatre in particular has always been a contentious art form that, especially in the last century, has let hardly any potential conflict lie. The direct attacks artists have launched against one another, from Futurists to Communists to Situationists, have

The so-called center of society clamors for the supposed artistic right to offend others, at the same time insisting that these others have no reason to be offended.

frequently been far more harsh than anything else happening at the moment. Often, instead of piling excitement on excitement, stopping to take a breath would be a better strategy. Taking a step back from one's own hurt feelings can also make it possible to understand things from vantages other than the here and now. There is a lot that is currently being negotiated, fought against and for. In the end, though, Maoism didn't take over after 1968, nor did free love become the new marriage. Political struggles are wars of position, strategic as well as emotional accelerations.

Identity Politics

Stumbling and Stuttering

The complex situation in which we find ourselves is an ideal context for an art whose task is not to make everything easier, but rather to open up new horizons, to confront our own ways of living and seeing with other viewpoints, to uncover our own entanglements in the political dilemmas of our time. The battle over images and words that is currently raging is an expression of a learning process taking place on all sides. There is much trial and error; it is difficult to foresee where the path—for the world, the West, politics, art—will lead. What was possible just a few years ago is now blowing up in our faces. But fear, petulance, and nostalgia are not good points of departure for making or receiving art. Better are curiosity, empathy, and courage.

> Taking a step back from one's own hurt feelings can also make it possible to understand things from vantages other than the here and now.

To complicate perception is an aesthetic strategy straight from the artist's basic toolbox: integrating hurdles, stumbling blocks, and confusions that interrupt the flow of experience and allow another reality to penetrate. "Much has been said about stuttering as error, about the blight of stuttering and about its limitations ... okay, but hardly anything about the advantages, about the gift of stuttering, about how it changes your perceptions, about the intuitive strength of observation, of feeling, towards oneself and the other..."[57] noted the late German director and author Einar Schleef, referring to more than his own speech impairment: a mental double take, a pause taken while reading, listening, watching, looking. The activation of one's own thinking; making breaks and gaps visible.

The feeling that speaking is becoming an increasingly complicated act is representative of all the current arenas of the struggle for representation and participation. To assume this to be unaesthetic would mean confusing aesthetics with sleek beauty. Perhaps today's interventions will have disappeared tomorrow. But perhaps, like much that once began as a stumbling block built into a work of art, we just won't notice them anymore.

In the case of the painting of the open coffin of the murdered Black boy Emmett Till described above, there was a form of protest that was more lasting and artistically more sophisticated than the demand for the work's destruction. Parker Bright, a Black US-American artist, expressed his criticism of Dana Schutz's painting through a performative act of interruption. He stood in front of the painting with his back to the audience, wearing a T-shirt printed with the text "Black Death Spectacle." The painting remained intact, the view was obstructed; it will be almost impossible to imagine the work in the future without this comment. Both perspectives continued to exist, but not separately from one another.

Antanas Mockus as "Super-Citizen"

PARTICIPATION

When Antanas Mockus became mayor of Bogotá in 1995, the city had a reputation as one of the most dangerous in the world, plagued by drugs, crime, corruption, and machismo. A philosopher, mathematician, and in many ways the opposite of a career politician, Mockus had campaigned without party support and literally without a budget, clinging to the belief that people could be convinced of the possibility of another world. His most important task once in office was, in his view, encouraging others to take control of their own lives with confidence while at the same time strengthening their sense of responsibility towards the society to which they belong. He invented the concept of *cultura ciudadana* (citizen culture): a kind of civil autodidactic practice based on play, symbolic acts, and staged situations.

But above all, according to curator Joanna Warsza, Mockus lived by his oft-repeated phrase, "When I am trapped, I try to do what an artist would do."[58] For him, using strategies of contemporary art meant decontextualizing everyday situations, framing them differently, making them graspable. And, at the same time, working in this way gave him a sense of freedom: the ability to see things in their complexity from a distance, thereby making change possible. He called his strategy *subart*: a modest art without symbolic pretensions, a way of borrowing from *high art* whatever could be useful and convertible into direct political action.[59]

Today, what Mockus accomplished during his tenure is legendary. He created a toys-for-firearms exchange (counting on kids putting pressure on their parents to make them give up their rifles and pistols); he had himself photographed in a "Super-Citizen" costume, both to make fun of his own supposed power and to show that, in a democracy, everyone can in principle acquire the legitimacy to govern. He cut a heart-shaped hole in his bulletproof vest, demonstrating his belief in nonviolence—and risking his life for real. In the most run-down parts of the city he founded libraries where books could be borrowed, without identification, on an honor system. To talk about violence and murder, he organized performances at open graves. He fired corrupt traffic cops and replaced them with over 400 mimes, knowing that for Colombians, the threat of ridicule was a better deterrent than any fine.[60]

And: he was unbelievably successful. Within three years, the number of traffic-related deaths fell by more than fifty percent and the number of homicides by more than seventy. In surveys, a large majority of the residents of Bogotá suddenly began to rate their city as worth living in, and 63,000 citizens voluntarily chose to pay an extra ten percent in taxes.[61]

Pantomime, heart-shaped cutouts, performances in cemeteries; all this might—by aesthetic standards like complexity and ambiguity—not really sound like particularly good theatre. And yet, when else has art had such an effect? Mockus' subart popularized strategies from theatre, performance, and conceptual art as a means of engaging the citizens of Bogotá in public life. For Mockus, participation meant sharing, not only power, but responsibility as well. His politics—and his art—proposed an alternative to the ongoing compulsion to participate in an *all-inclusive* capitalism, which, contrary to what Marx predicted, has through affirmation been able to resolve its internal contradictions thus far. Mockus refused to accept the post-political condition in which participation had become a pure sedative with the sinister side effect of shifting responsibility onto citizens who do not have much influence over the outcomes. In which occasional elections, a barebones social safety net, a few measures against climate change and human rights violations, and a handful of cultural adornments are enough to ease our collective conscience.

The theatrical equivalent of this post-political situation is so-called participatory theatre, in which participation is more often than not a placebo, purporting to hand over decisions to the audience that are actually long predetermined. Audiences end up compelled to participate in a transparent fraud. The problem is not so much being forced into participation, the problem is being forced into *feigned* participation. Thus, although our involvement in society and art is constant, it is mostly only as consumers of goods and entertainment in a world full of so-called experiences that distract us from demanding actual influence. This is passivity disguised as activity.

> **The problem is not so much being forced into participation, the problem is being forced into *feigned* participation.**

But as problematic as the term participation may have become or have been made: if theatre wants to be political, it has to get right to the middle of the dilemma and confront what it could mean to take part. The question is not just how to avoid false, surface-level participation devoid of meaning. The point is to take back the idea of real participation, to give it meaning again, to sound out its radical potential.

Bertolt Brecht's *Lehrstücke* (learning plays) were meant to be performed by the audience—in this case, the working class—itself and thus dissolve the separation between auditorium and stage, which has been around at least since the mid-nineteenth century, when the bourgeois theatre turned off the house lights. By making different standpoints visible within a concrete argument, Brecht's dialectical theatre wanted to enable the audience to understand the system behind such debates instead of identifying too easily with a prescribed opinion. Beginning in the 1970s, Brazilian theatremaker

Augusto Boal, with his Theatre of the Oppressed (TO), built on this idea by handing over the responsibility even for the development of the whole performance to the "spect-actors" (a term combining spectator with actor, reflecting the way his technique dissolves the separation between these roles). In various formats like Forum Theatre, Invisible Theatre, and Legislative Theatre, the social and political realities of those gathered are playfully examined, with the clear aim (expressed in his terminology "rehearsal of revolution"[62]) of changing these very realities. Especially in Africa and parts of South America, Boal's approach is to this day among the most widespread and effective forms of theatre, becoming even more common in recent years. The fact that Forum Theatre in particular (in which audience members can tag in to play a character, or add a new one) is now often used by NGOs that are close to the system, with professional troupes and predetermined questions, also shows its limits: instead of rehearsing for the revolution, the aim becomes to quietly solve problems that those who finance or initiate the Forum Theatre in question have created in the first place.[63]

In a certain sense, the early works of the German feminist theatre collective She She Pop, around the year 2000, can also be read as postmodern learning play adaptations. The metanarratives had been lost, and society had splintered into small communities of interest. What remained was the sense that one could only learn from one's own stories. She She Pop put themselves and their audience at the center; everything revolved around questions of self-representation, self-exposure, and shame. Anyone who came had to take part; "just watching" was impossible. And the discomfort of participation was always just as important as the pleasure of it:

> Yes, I think, here we all are. The circle of chairs has filled up, that's nice to see. There are some new faces this time. Some still look a little unsure. Perhaps this is the right moment for all of us to make

a pact, each of us with ourselves, that says everything that will happen to us tonight is okay.[64]

This new kind of theatrical pact is deceptive. It is only you yourself who gives the assurance that everything that will happen is okay; there is no guarantee made on the part of the artists: "The relationship between the performers and the audience is not equal. There is a limit on the audience's freedom to act. But when it does become possible, it isn't denied; everyone experiences it."[65]

Even if such turn-of-the-century struggles with self-actualization now seem oddly autoreferential and navel-gazing, a problem specific to Generation X, the way that She She Pop tested out a new tone of speaking with the audience has helped in shifting what is possible for the theatre. Unlike the roughly contemporaneous emergence of relational aesthetics in the visual arts, which focused on relationships between people and on the social context but celebrated them primarily as friendly togetherness, artists like She She Pop pulled down their pants metaphorically and sometimes for real. The private was made public, up to the limits of pain and embarrassment.

The often literal parlor game dramaturgy of She She Pop's performances that "were more like *games* than *plays*"[66] shows how central the question of artistic and social rules is for all forms of participatory art. As curator Nora Sternfeld writes, though in a different context: "So what is at stake are the rules of the game themselves."[67]

One project that consistently illuminates this is *Building Conversation* by Dutch theatremaker Lotte van den Berg, which has been ongoing since 2014. On the shoulders of Brecht and Boal, she distills theatre to what she sees as its essence: a place of meeting and communication, where conflicts can be pointed out and experienced. An agreement made to engage in an exchange, according to certain rules, which may differ depending on the occasion.

So, *Building Conversation* is just that: people talking with one another. After showing your ticket at the theatre, you are taken, with the rest of the audience, to a place in the city: an apartment, a studio, an empty room... . Someone explains the rules; in some conversations, everyone agrees beforehand on the duration of the evening or on a topic. And then you are left with an obligation that is hard to shake off since leaving such a small group, refusing the exercise, is difficult. Whether you want to or not, you share the responsibility for the evening—its success or failure—whatever you consider to be the criteria.

Inspired by conversation techniques from all over the world, van den Berg has developed models and frames for dialogues in which there are no actors, no audience, only the invitation to participate, for example, in a wordless conversation or in a format developed by Jesuits, alternating between reflection, withdrawal, and dialogue. Another conversation completely dispenses with moderation, topic, or goal, a method that was developed by quantum physicist David Bohm to sound out patterns of collective thinking. *Building Conversation* relates directly to Chantal Mouffe's concept of agonistic pluralism; one of the conversations is dedicated to her approach.

What makes these conversations theatre is nothing more than the agreement to understand them as theatre. An agreement that enables us to be engaged while maintaining analytical distance. Who speaks how and what they say, who is silent, who is bored, who is interesting... . Sometimes it doesn't take more than a few precise decisions, gestures, and rules to mark out an area of art and to open up a wide playing field for possible experiences.

Care and Confrontation

The increase in participatory and politically engaged art since the 1990s is also referred to as the social turn. British art historian Claire

Bishop, even as she coins this term in her influential book *Artificial Hells*, simultaneously makes it clear that we really should be talking about a *re*-turn. After all, many of the ideas and methods can be found in some form throughout the entire twentieth century, but especially in the 1960s and 1970s:

> The artist is conceived less as an individual producer of discrete objects than as a collaborator and producer of situations; the work of art as a finite, portable, commodifiable product is reconceived as an ongoing or long-term project with an unclear beginning and end; while the audience, previously conceived as a "viewer" or "beholder", is now repositioned as a co-producer or participant. [68]

It is no coincidence that this sounds reminiscent of strategies used in postdramatic theatre. Bishop herself, though not especially interested in theatre as such, is explicit about her desire to describe, and rethink, the history of participatory visual arts through a theatrical lens.[69] What is added to the postdramatic postulate, however, is an ethical claim with a clear political demand: the situations referred to above are not purely or even primarily aesthetic, but social. They gesture beyond the work of art.

Participation in art can serve to examine or develop models for sharing power and responsibility differently, and in this way sound out new forms of participation for larger social contexts. On the other hand, it can also consciously problematize participation, playing with abuse of power in such a fashion that the audience-participants' discomfort enables (or forces) them to reach a new understanding.

This is quite a tightrope to walk, because art answers the question of the responsibility towards its participants differently than activism or social work do. When Claire Bishop describes participatory art as a genre in which "people constitute the central artistic medium and material,"[70] she assigns a clear object status to audience-participants that activists, for example, would be highly unlikely to use when outlining their approach.

Art, however, can also aim at direct confrontation or experiment with misunderstanding; it can seduce, manipulate, or even put pressure on its audience and through this establish a counterpoint to the friendly consensus that many politically intended artworks assume. The works of Spanish artist Santiago Sierra, for example, are known for their conceptual and minimalist clarity, but above all for the disturbing extremes with which Sierra uses people as material: paying them minimal wages for obviously pointless, humiliating actions such as when he had a line tattooed across the backs of six young Cubans in front of a running camera (*250 cm Line Tattooed on 6 Paid People*, 1999). A year later, in a radicalized version of the same basic concept, he used heroin as currency to pay four drug-addicted sex workers. By reproducing injustice, financial dependency, and (mostly Western) societies' abuse of power within the frame of his works, Sierra repeats the despised mechanisms in order to criticize them.

Dutch artist Renzo Martens used a similar strategy in his early film *Enjoy Poverty* (2008), showing how he convinces Congolese photographers to make a living by supplying Western media outlets with all the dire news from Africa they crave. Instead of weddings and other celebrations, they began to photograph war, or more precisely, "raped women, corpses, and, let's add, malnourished children."[71] The argument is crystal clear, rational—and deeply disturbing because it points right at our own Western hypocrisy.

The artist and theoretician Pablo Helguera differentiates between nonvoluntary (involving no negotiation or consent), voluntary (with a clear agreement, or even contract, as in Sierra's case), and involuntary participation, whose subtle, indirect negotiations are shaped by hidden agendas and in which "deceit and seduction play a central role."[72] While in Sierra's work there is a clear-cut deal with the participants (not that this makes things more pleas-

She She Pop: *Oratorium*

ant), in Martens' film it is not at all obvious to what degree those involved grasp the implications of the work. This extends to the artist himself, who puts himself right in the middle of the action instead of sitting safely on the outside.

Much of Polish artist Artur Żmijewski's work is even more provocative; his protagonists (to apply Helguera's definition) "at first willingly engage but later become involuntary participants or actors."[73] In Żmijewski's video *80064* (2004), Holocaust survivor Jozef Tarnawa is not literally forced into having the faded concentration camp identification number re-tattooed; but it is obvious that he only endures the procedure after heavy persuasion.

None of these works is offering concrete suggestions for change. Their aim is to reveal what society would prefer to sweep under the carpet; they offer no easy answers, nor do they lead to cathartic relief. They shift the weight from the ambiguity of the artwork to the ambiguity of our own lives.

But in these actions by Sierra, Żmijewski, and Martens, there are, unlike in theatre, no spectators present during the process itself. Those involved, however voluntarily, are the "material" of the work but not intended as its primary recipients. The resulting moral dilemma is an essential part of the effect. When artists like Sierra, Żmijewski, or Martens deny us the position of neutral viewer and force us into the role of witness, they are making a gesture with a long history—from Brecht's "Stop staring so romantically" banners addressing the audience in *Drums in the Night* (1922) to US-American performance artist Chris Burden's legendary performance *Shoot* (1971), in which he had a friend shoot him at close range in his left arm with a rifle, transforming the audience into witnesses in both an artistic and legal sense.

But we are not good, nor neutral, witnesses: simply by being present (and not intervening), we legitimize what is happening, even

> **Such works shift the weight from the ambiguity of the artwork to the ambiguity of our own lives.**

make it possible in the first place. We become accomplices. And voyeurs, too, if we don't walk out. There is something illicit about our gaze. But even as voyeurs we are not particularly good; how are we supposed to relish in secret pleasure when the whole point is to show us how audacious it is that we're looking at all? In the end, we are just as bad witnesses as we are voyeurs. And suddenly we find ourselves to be the ones actually accused.

Art theorist Irit Rogoff suggests that participation could also mean looking the other way, and by doing so, freeing ourselves from what artists or curators have planned for us.[74] But while that may be a good way to escape annoying, enforced participation shoved on us by an artist, it does not free us from responsibility for the evils at which we're choosing not to look.

> **In the end, we are just as bad witnesses as we are voyeurs. And suddenly we find ourselves to be the ones actually accused.**

This is why it is almost impossible not to be disturbed by the works of Sierra, Żmijewski, or Martens; the dilemma of our gaze does not resolve on the second, or even the third, viewing. This is strong artistic work. This is political work that refers without doubt to real social problems. And the questions it raises are complex, not easily resolved. Simply rejecting this work as immoral would be too simplistic, and so would ethically acquitting it. But as productive as this line of inquiry may be, the fact remains that these artists are consciously choosing to be part of the problem and not the solution. In order to point to a greater evil, they stick their fingers into the wound of representation, thus repeating injustice much more than symbolically; they in fact create it themselves, in the concrete situations they establish.

At the other end of the participation spectrum stand artists who are primarily guided by empathy, who place care and often humility at the center of their work. Mierle Laderman Ukeles, a US-American feminist artist, invented the genre of Maintenance Art at the end of the 1960s when as a young mother she was confronted with the fact that supporting and maintaining another living being, while it had suddenly become her main occupation, was not recognized from the outside as "real" work. Needless to say, the male artists she admired at the time did not have to contend with such challenges: "I am a woman. I am a wife. I am a mother (random order). I do a hell of a lot of washing, cleaning, cooking, renewing, supporting, preserving, etc. Also, (up to now separately) I 'do' Art. Now, I will simply do these everyday things, and flush them up to consciousness, exhibit them, as Art."[75] With her *Manifesto for Maintenance Art 1969!* Ukeles brought everyday activities connected with support, upkeep, and care, along with maintenance, cleaning, etc., into the limelight—activities that make it possible to live (and make art) in a society in the first place, but which, as a rule, do not have public visibility ("after the revolution, who's going to pick up the garbage on Monday morning?"[76]). In her legendary piece *Touch Sanitation* (1977–80), she shook hands with all 8,500 employees of New York City's Department of Sanitation and thanked them for their work. Today she is still, as she has been for more than forty years, the unpaid artist-in-residence in the municipal sanitation department.

The Hungarian-Dutch theatremaker Edit Kaldor also grapples with questions that society prefers to avoid, addressing issues such as child abuse or death. For her, the point is not an artistic test of courage in mastering a subject that cannot actually be mastered: on the contrary, it is to make oneself vulnerable. Her work often begins just at the juncture at which it seems impossible to go on, at which you feel helpless.

The Inventory of Powerlessness (2013–16) is a collection of such moments. Brief stories from participants compiled anew in each city stand alongside spontaneous contributions from the audience, in front of a diagram of powerlessness projected on the wall: psychotic breaks, episodes of incarceration, illnesses, miscarriages, the process of seeking asylum, are linked with more mundane experiences—not categorized, but brought into relation. "Instead of the tried and true models of power structures, a network of powerlessness emerges."[77]

Yet for Kaldor, powerlessness is not necessarily a negative term. While approaches that portray the powerless as victims often just reinforce the feeling of a lack of control, *Inventory* is not about pity, but about recognition, sympathy, perhaps understanding. And above all, it is about getting in touch with yourself and recognizing experiences of powerlessness as part of your own life.

Safer Spaces, Braver Spaces

There is a clear trend now to exhibit one's own wounds, trauma, or shame onstage. Joseph Beuys' motto "Show your wound," which the late director Christoph Schlingensief—who exposed his own suffering from terminal cancer with shocking honesty in his last performances—used to quote frequently, has become the leitmotif for a generation of theatremakers. Programs like the ones put together by the SICK! Festival in Manchester or the Basler Dokumentartage (Basel Documentary Platform) show how the theatre can be turned into a protected place, and an opportunity for the audience to experience something that they might otherwise never encounter: disturbing insights as they are shared by British artist and activist James Leadbitter, also known as The Vacuum Cleaner, in his solo *Mental* (2013), an autobiographical piece in which he uses psychiatric records and police files to tell the story of his fight against the violence of being institutionalized as a borderline patient.

Such approaches understand the theatre at least partly as a sanctuary, as a safe space (or at least a "safer space" to follow today's preferred terminology)—a concept that has its origins in the USA in the 1960s, where it first appeared in the context of the feminist movement and was later taken up by civil rights activists: a protected space in which a group of people who already had the short end of the stick could come together to define their own goals and strategies without being constantly challenged. It was a matter of having a say in the first place; of formulating common goals, but also discussing how these could be achieved without shying away from disagreement.

In this context also belong the trigger warnings that more and more often preface a visit to the theatre: indications that certain content, images, or ways of speaking that may be offensive or disturbing to some of the audience are to be expected on stage. While there have long been warnings against nudity or "explicit language" in the USA, more notices have become standard in recent years, primarily for depictions or themes of racism, sexual and other violence, and discriminatory language.

Trigger as a term comes from trauma therapy, which holds that certain stimuli—topics, words, situations—can trigger a traumatic memory and possibly even lead to re-traumatization. It's quite recently that the concept has propagated outward from trauma therapy, often in tandem with the demand for safe spaces, above all to North American universities, Internet forums, activist circles and, eventually, artists.[78]

As important as it is to protect people against insult, injury, and re-traumatization, the broad demand to turn theatres, museums, and universities generally into safer spaces, harbors the risk of self-segregation. The group to which you feel you belong—not to mention, the group to which others perceive you as belonging—keeps shrinking. One of the attempts to escape from this trap is the proposal to establish "brave spaces" parallel to safe spaces, spaces where there are no limits to freedom of expression, where everything can be discussed openly and radically.[79] An agonistic arena, which is clearly defined in terms of space, time, and participants.

Works like *Inventory* play with the productive paradoxes of theatre in a different way. They are safe spaces and spaces of discomfort at the same time. The safety guaranteed on the stage does not apply to the auditorium, whose supposedly stable ground of normality begins to sway for some viewers, confronted as they are with vulnerable bodies, naked shame, and demands that are often not easy to digest.

We can also see Ann Liv Young's evil clown in this context: the extreme therapy sessions the US-American performer offers in the character of blond-wigged, buxom Sherry from the deep South rely on confusion and direct confrontation. There are no safe spaces here, especially for the public. Never missing a beat, Young takes her vis-à-vis hostage by means that are at first humorous and playful before they become unpleasant and intentionally embarrassing. She pushes all of the limits, from those of taste and aesthetics to psychological and even sometimes physical ones. When she picks out her interlocutors—or better, victims—and asks them in front of an assembled audience (that tends to duck away) questions about their sexuality, their suspected macho tendencies, or other intimate details, smart comebacks don't do much to help them out of the mess. In this group therapy, Sherry clearly has the upper hand. Getting too close—physically and mentally—is the program. And self-discovery, as she says in an accompanying text, is "not an option, but an order."[80]

> **Such works are safe spaces and spaces of discomfort at the same time. The safety guaranteed on the stage does not apply to the auditorium.**

At the same time there is never any doubt: this is theatre, from the wig to the persona. You can leave at any time—but it's unlikely it will go unnoticed. In order not to grant her (after all, usually rather liberal and reasonably prepared) audience the trivial sense of benign approval, Sherry sometimes overshoots the target, allowing her Southern character to adopt racist appropriations[81] or provoking open disputes and prematurely broken-off shows.[82] Ann Liv Young always exposes herself to the situation, staying vulnerable throughout her performance.

The fact that an artificial alter ego only provides limited protection is also pointed out by Julia*n Meding as the title character in Swiss theatremaker Boris Nikitin's *Hamlet* (2016): "This isn't theatre. And it's not real life!" The boards this Hamlet treads as he delivers his grand (and reproachful, combative, plaintive) soliloquy do mean the world—and nothing at all. With a slinking gait, excluded but still at the center—manic, depressive, extroverted, introverted, always too much, too close, always too real, too strong, too fragile—performer and musician Meding shows us a person who, like the great Shakespearean model, is more prickly than he is sympathetic or conciliatory. A poetic revolutionary: in one moment raw, confrontational, anti-social, in the next he does an about-face, appeasingly seeking understanding. Meding's Hamlet is not Shakespeare's Prince of Denmark: he hardly speaks a word of the famous original and yet he is a prototypical, in many regards non-binary Hamlet for our times. To be or not to be, to prevaricate or to act, to belong or to remain aloof: here it is no longer a question of making a decision, but rather of tensions that must be withstood.

Few other works by Nikitin get under the skin quite so much as this account of illness, death, depression, of wanting to be different and having to be different. The role and character we presume to be real melt into each other, theatrical reflections and existential questions about life fuse, when, accompanied by a live baroque quartet, Meding exposes his body and (what appears to be) his biography to the scrutiny of the audience, treading a fine line between performance and theatrical illusion, between outgoing dilettantism and an actor's virtuosity.

This Hamlet—not unlike James Leadbitter in *Mental* with his self-referentiality and troubled mind—doesn't make things easy

for us. He accuses us as well as himself, often unjustly and self-righteously so. He is brave, not complacent, but he is also annoying; he demands that his audience constantly examine and re-examine its position.

There are no clear, predictable boundaries to be drawn between projects that use care and those whose strategy is based on dissent. The underlying motivation is often as similar as the approach is different. Many works that play with confrontation or even antagonism are at the same time expressions of deep compassion, a cry insisting that attention must be paid to the misery of the world. However empathic or confrontational a work of art may be, in the end, according to Pablo Helguera, it is wrong to "create a division between controversial or confrontational works and nonconfrontational ones. Antagonism is not a genre but rather a quality of artmaking that is simply more exacerbated in some practices than others."[83]

Participation Behind the Scenes

The processes through which art is produced are themselves political. That is why making political theatre requires, in no small way, questioning one's own working conditions and structures. It isn't enough to call for a different society onstage; we must look offstage for corresponding new forms of cooperation and new ways of doing. This has at last become a commonly stated position, but putting it into practice is another question. And this is not only due to bigotry or simple laziness. To challenge and alter hierarchies and the distribution of power, whether at the institutional level or in the context of a single production, is not a task that can be completed quickly. In addition to very different interests, administrative and technical processes also play a role, as do entrenched artistic ideas and routines.

The few but legendary attempts at co-determination in Germany's municipal theatres (primarily in the 1970s) were short-lived and are now mostly dismissed as a failed exercise—not infrequently with the patriarchal explanation that the actors themselves were the ones who wanted to return the directors to a position of power, and that many of them were not able to cope with the psychological stress caused, for example, by a public discussion of how to distribute roles. However, what most thoroughly put the idea to rest was the oft repeated, no matter how poorly founded, argument that art is intrinsically not democratic. Even if in-house hierarchies and working conditions in many theatres have recently been aggressively questioned: to this day few of the artists employed by municipal theatres or other venues have even a partial say when it comes to the conditions under which their work is created.

More than most venues want to admit, such structural realities also influence the artistic results. Not only do necessity and tradition shape the rigid processes, working hours, and habits of administrative and technical routines, but also the artistic vision itself. Many independent theatre groups emerged not least as a reaction to this. Their search for alternative aesthetic approaches was inseparable from the search for alternative forms of collaboration.

For the handful of female students at the Institute for Applied Theatre Studies in Giessen, Germany, who founded the performance collective She She Pop in the early 1990s, it was far from insignificant that directing, as a field, was still overwhelmingly male. Their formation followed an impulse that was clearly "political and feminist"; the goal was

> to shake off patriarchal and hierarchical modes of production, assert a different reality for the stage, and promote an alternative mode of production.... This mode of production proposes that everyone is equally involved in decision-making processes for a given project,

> and that everyone performs the same tasks in solidarity with one another, each in their own way. Everyone should be able to identify with the end product in the same way and profits from it should be shared and managed collectively.[84]

Pragmatism and professionalization, and the compromises they demand, have without question left their marks on She She Pop over its more than 25 years of existence (certain administrative tasks, for example, are in fact delegated to individuals). However, organization and finances remain integrated with the collective's artistic activities, and the principle of interchangeability in administrative matters as well as onstage has both aesthetic consequences and an effect on group politics. When, for example, a piece tours with a changing line-up, that also changes the relationship with the audience, as founding member Ilia Papatheodorou writes:

> What's possible for me, what I perform, someone else has to be able to do, too. That makes the artistic authority I have in relation to the audience relatively minor.... . By making myself *equal to*, presenting my position onstage as an interchangeable one, I abolish myself.... . In this way I open up a gap inside of the work. I make it possible for many to break the work down, to connect to it; what I can do, they can, too.[85]

Even if the respective performers may be interchangeable within the collective's productions, the artistic style developed over years is not, and nor are the idiosyncrasies of individual members: "Our art consists in asking a question that no one person can answer alone. We disagree, and for us, that makes things richer."[86] As a collective, She She Pop maintains an identity that, while consistent, can be expanded time and time again, and the constellation of people out of which it is composed can open up and shift.

She She Pop has become a point of reference for many younger German theatremakers not only for artistic reasons (and not just because the group still exists after 25 years while other similar groups have long since left the precarious independent theatre scene). Equally important has been that the performers have never stopped addressing onstage the struggles inherent in their collective work and group dynamics. Maintaining horizontality, within the group itself but also in terms of how they are perceived from the outside, is not easy.

Over time, the independent theatre landscape has become characterized by very different constellations of collaboration that cannot be broken down into individual protagonists and job profiles. In addition, there are numerous duos and trios of directors who (in some cases, also as life partners) try out ways of working predicated on equal rights and blur the borders between creative and interpretive artists. In a shift that is slow and mostly free of too much ideological baggage, the romantic idea of the lone artistic genius is being replaced by more cooperative models.

Immersion: Participation as Submission

As a supposed variant of participatory art, the concept of immersion is currently highly traded in theatre, immersion here referring to the way the audience gets enfolded in an alternate reality in which any mark of an exterior is supposed to completely disappear. While the examples of participatory theatre described so far are defined by the fact that they can be experienced as reality and fiction at the same time, immersive theatre aims to achieve the totalizing experience of an artificial world that is endless, at least for those who do not try to open the doors at the edges of these expanded stages. Anyone who questions the rules here is just a bad sport.

Immersive theatre is often, but by no means always, interactive or participatory. (Interaction mostly refers to a one-to-one encounter, participation rather to a group.) Above all, however, it is strictly illusionistic, striving for verisimilitude with a singlemindedness of which Stanislavski would not have dared to dream.

Its historical roots can be found—depending on your preference—in intoxicated rituals, in the neo-Dionysian theatrical ecstasies of Antonin Artaud, and in the illusion machines of the Baroque that anticipate cinema. Or obviously in Stanislavski, even though immersive theatre's version of the "fourth wall," a device originally intended to enable unobserved observation, in a paradoxical move now includes the audience openly in the space of the performance.

But also, the Happening artists of the 1960s, above all the US-American action artist Allan Kaprow with his longing for an art that one steps into instead of looking at it from the outside, are cited as role models for immersion—even though they declared war on all illusionistic art forms.

For the theatre, the concept of immersion harbors two fundamental problems; one lies in the nature of the medium and its technical possibilities, the other in its political implications.

Just as the invention of film and the triumph of cinema pushed illusionistic theatre to its limits at the beginning of the twentieth century, recent developments in virtual reality techniques make immersive theatre look old before it has even had the chance to mature, which is perhaps one reason that there are so many immersive theatre pieces indulging a retro chic. Anyone who is looking for actual total entertainment is a lot more likely to get their money's worth with VR glasses or drug-based rituals than from being surrounded by wobbly theatrical illusions.

The more ethically sensitive issue has to do with the political implications of a manipulative totality. Immersion demands that its audiences surrender to an artistic vision or even to an ideology; it relies on the strategy of shock and awe. There is no room for the "emancipated spectator" in such a tightly constructed work. Immersion forces participation without reflection and without political awareness.

Boris Nikitin: *Hamlet*

The problem becomes clear with the likely world record-holder of immersive art, Russian filmmaker Ilya Khrzhanovsky's large-scale film, performance, and art spectacle *DAU* (since 2009), which is dedicated to the life of Soviet physicist Lev Davidovich Landau.

The project was first and foremost immersive for those involved in its three-year filming: an enormous film set was built in Kharkov, Ukraine, a creative reconstruction of the Soviet Academy of Sciences' ominous, and secret, Institute for Physical Problems as it was from 1938 to 1968. Hundreds of actors and philosophers, artists and mystics, scientists and cooks, nurses and hairdressers were installed there to enact a 24/7 continuous role play, their costumed routine a re-enactment of the imagined everyday life of the institute surrounding the legendary physicist. Day and night they experienced "real," i.e., immersive conditions, including violence, drinking, and a few pregnancies.

> **Immersive theatre aims to achieve the totalizing experience of an artificial world that is endless, at least for those who do not try to open the doors at the edges of these expanded stages.**

The intent was for the total experience that the performers had had to be felt by audiences when they were shown extracts from the 700 hours' worth of filmed material. In conjunction with the showing in Berlin, Khrzhanovsky had planned to reconstruct part of the Berlin Wall. After a long back and forth, this was prevented (officially, at least) by security concerns. Instead, a smaller version of the spectacle took place in Paris at the beginning of 2019, where the film material was also presented for the first time.

DAU makes the political implications of immersive art particularly clear not only due to the project's massive size, but also to its thematically inevitable flirtation with Stalinist aesthetics.* But

---

* It is important to mention, though, that Ilya Khrzhanovsky has distanced himself clearly from Putin's authoritarianism, even long before the Russian invasion of Ukraine.

even with ideologically more harmless work, there is often less than a breath between immersion and drowning. These projects are not about emancipation and knowledge, but about submission. There is not much left of the "individualized spaces of experience"[87] which art theorist Dorothea von Hantelmann emphatically seeks in immersion.

Allan Kaprow himself, as it happens, made it very clear that being *in* a work of art should not mean forgetting the outside: "The situations for a happening should come from what you see in the real world, from real places and people rather than from the head. If you stick to imagination too much you'll end up with old art again, since art was always supposed to be made from imagination."[88]

Occupy Wall Street

ART AND ACTIVISM

Tunisia, Egypt, Spain, Portugal, Greece. A little later New York, London, Tel Aviv, and Istanbul, then Brazil, Japan, Korea, Argentina... the year 2010 kicked off a decade of demonstrations all around the world. The catalysts igniting each instance of unrest may differ, but artists were and are almost always among the first to take up the call for social justice and strengthened democracy. No matter the site (squares and parks like Tahrir, Zuccotti, Syntagma, Taksim, and Maidan), no matter the backdrop (Tokyo after Fukushima, Niemeyer's iconic parliamentary architecture in Brasilia, or beneath umbrellas in Hong Kong), the same question could be found: how could art, how could artistic strategies and tactics, play a relevant role in these movements?

In contrast to art, political activism usually has clarified the reasons, commitments, and goals of an action in advance. Additionally, it often features a consequent straightforwardness, uncompromised devotion, and sophisticated strategies for collective work and participation. No wonder many politically committed artists and cultural workers regard political activists around the world with a measure of respect. The political theatre of recent years, therefore, can hardly be understood without taking a look at this connection.[89]

Art and politics have always had an intense love-hate relationship. Artists have positioned themselves in relation to power somewhere between servile followers and aloof critics, between constructive cooperators and tough antagonists. It is no coincidence that artistic methods and even definitions of what art can and should be often develop or radicalize during periods of social upheaval. These are moments in which the relationship between art and society in general is at a turning point: immediately before and after the First World War (Dada, Futurism, Constructivism), in the 1960s and early 1970s (performance art, conceptual art, installation art). They are moments for an artistic and philosophical, but also a political, avant-garde.

So it is not surprising that politically and socially engaged art got a fresh boost after 1989, with the collapse of the Eastern Bloc, the end of the Cold War, the acceleration of capitalism, and the accompanying rise of anti-globalization movements. But it is only in the context of the various political and economic crises of recent years that the genre "activist art" has become a widespread phenomenon.

A wide range of new or renewed alliances between art and activism have emerged. Some are so close that they have fused into a unified concept, art activism, sometimes even styled as a single word: artivism. By emphasizing the desire to use artistic skills, tools, and strategies to achieve activist goals, this term unites somewhat strange bedfellows. Where artists refuse to forego complexity and ambiguity, activists tend to despise such ambivalence as well as the traditional role of artists as sole authors, and even more their entanglement in the art market.

At the core of activism stands the concept of direct action: an action with the very concrete goal of pointing out a problem, showing an alternative, or even a possible solution. Direct action can be violent or explicitly non-violent. Strikes in any form might be direct actions, as well as occupations, acts of civil disobedience or resistance, sabotages, blockades, attacks, and assaults. Online interventions are included, too, such as hacking. The word "direct" refers to the idea of immediacy; the time to talk and negotiate is over, or at least interrupted. Direct action is the opposite of hesitation, of ambivalence. Reflection is, to a degree, deferred. In this sense, direct action seems to be the moment when activism is furthest away from art.

On the other hand, there is also the moment when a performance gains momentum, when it reaches its point of no return. When it is all about the here and now. In this sense, direct action seems to be the moment when activism is closest to art. Many radical moments in performance art or live art can easily be described as direct action.

Just like live art, direct action is not spontaneous. Preparation and staging are often meticulous. Various possible developments are considered and potential encounters, stumbling blocks, mistakes, and chance are anticipated. Planning a direct action is much like planning a military action—or a piece of performance art. Pussy Riot did not just storm Moscow's Cathedral of Christ the Savior in February 2012 and then spontaneously decide what to do. They chose the setting carefully, rehearsing the text and choreography of their "Punk Prayer." This tight preparation was necessary so that when the time came, the all-female group of performers could deliver the performance for a brief forty seconds in front of the altar, a place where women are forbidden.[90] Yekaterina Samutsevich, one of the key protagonists, explains that often several weeks are necessary to prepare for such actions: to discuss topics, write songs, and develop site-specific performances. Who will constitute the audience (including security guards)? Where are the entrances and exits? How long will the performance be? Documentation, which is also painstakingly planned, is then edited and posted on the Internet as an integral part of the work.[91]

Definitions of what art can and should be often develop or radicalize during periods of social upheaval.

The final performance happens in conditions that cannot be simulated in advance; a dress rehearsal is not possible, neither are repeat performances. In this respect, direct action not only resembles certain forms of performance art, but also experimental approaches like those of the Belgian theatre group TG Stan, that used to sit around a table for weeks discussing, interpreting, and going over the piece they planned to perform—but only at the evening of the premiere did they actually get up and perform together.

Even the radical anarchists who made up the Russian art-activist group Voina had to prepare extensively for their legendary 2010 action, in which they painted a 65-meter erect penis on the side of St. Petersburg's Liteyny drawbridge. When the bridge was raised, as it was every night, the phallus pointed squarely in the direction of the headquarters of the Federal Security Service of the Russian Federation FSB (formerly the KGB).

Just as artists and theatremakers have been inspired by the numerous political movements of recent years and seek to bring some of this momentum into their work, activists' repertoires have long included strategies borrowed from the theatre.

For example, the London-based Clandestine Insurgent Rebel Clown Army (C.I.R.C.A.), "armed with mockery and love,"[92] has since 2003 used theatrical means to cause confusion and defuse tensions in heated confrontations between demonstrators and police, in Great Britain and elsewhere. Especially in the early days, the clowns, trained by professionals, actually succeeded again and again in breaking insurmountable lines held by riot police thanks to their playful interventions because "the cops were laughing too much to concentrate."[93]

But here the same can be said of all direct action: it is only successful when executed well, as John Jordan, one of the founders of the Clown Army and an influential artivist, points out:

> Rebel clowns are not meant to *pretend* to be clowns, they should be real clowns and like all arts this requires practice and dedica-

tion... . The urgency of activism meant that many activists never took the time to really train in the art of clowning and as a result many bad "hippy" clowns ended up on the streets, thinking that being in the Clown Army was just about dressing up, rather than a deep physical and psychological practice that could lead to effective direct action.[94]

Reverend Billy, too, has a lot of experience with coming into immediate contact with the authorities. About twenty years ago he stood alone in New York's Times Square, a cross between an Elvis impersonator and charismatic televangelist, preaching with a full voice against consumer capitalism and destruction of the environment. Since then, the fictional character developed by US-American actor, action artist, and activist William Talen has, together with his partner Savitri D., gathered around fifty musicians, performers, and singers into their community. The Church of Stop Shopping appropriates the aesthetics and rhetoric of US-American televangelism, which provide an ideological foundation for, primarily, the extreme right. Using their own versions of gospel songs and breathless, playfully eloquent sermons, Reverend Billy, Savitri D., and the Stop Shopping Choir turn the tables on the genre. They transform its hallmarks (eleventh-hour threats of hell leveled against all those perceived as different, hysterical patriotism, and romanticization of the USA as the promised land) into a call to fight for love and resist the impending climate catastrophe. They maintain the tension between parody and firm belief in their "post-religious" church, using community centers, crosswalks, forests, parking lots, shopping malls, and bank lobbies as their stages, as well as theatres and concert halls. Alongside these in-person appearances, they reach a global audience with feature-length documentaries and, above all, countless YouTube clips.

The idea of the community that supports this "church" is just as real as its leader, the false reverend, is fictional. Join the choir in the shabby basement rehearsal room of a seedy Lower East Side

Reverend Billy

community center and its diversity is readily apparent. Its constituents are mixed (not only in gender, skin color, and age, but also in social background) to a degree that few other theatre projects are able to attain. Here, ethics and aesthetics are one. What is preached is also collectively lived.

In the context of social and political movements such as Occupy Wall Street, the Church of Stop Shopping offers both a concise form for direct action and a medium for formulating common concerns in a public manner and bringing campaigns to the news. The venerable Billy and his comrades-in-arms preach at Occupy Wall Street, storm Starbucks and Victoria's Secret. They perform exorcisms of ATMs in the lobbies of banks, but also of the Tate Modern in London to purge it of sponsorship by oil giant and environmental sinner BP: "Earthalujah!"

> I am in love with preaching. [The US-American performance artist and musician] Laurie Anderson has called it the "crack between talking and singing." I would call it the landscape between, the dreamland beyond. The vowels can howl full of breath, the consonants stop suddenly to deliver a hostage-taking silence... .
>
> In an activist event, say the takeover of a bank lobby, we believe that the collision of my right wing threads and left wing voice—and the intimidating presence of the Stop Shopping Choir in their fervent harmonies—release powerfully upon the customers, tellers, rent-a-cops, and the bank manager. I'm told that, as the singing and preaching about the bank's behavior gets under way, that people have trouble focusing on what's happening. The whole thing is too jarring, with the gospel concert and radical lyrics and the Elvis impersonator out front ... and we find that the inability to place us easily in a category requires that each witness figure out in a more original way than they might otherwise what we are, and who they are, and just what this bank is doing... .[95]

Theatrical forms are used here to create confusion, to interrupt perceptions. But this is not an end in itself, nor is it meant to be enough on its own as a political gesture. Instead, the aim is to bring—for a brief moment, in a specific place (with a symbolic meaning)—the march of capitalism to a standstill. And, perhaps, to open in this sudden interruption space for reflection. Whether we have followed the choir down the street or have been surprised by it in a bank, if we do not turn away, we become accomplices through sheer presence. The rhythm of everyday life skips a beat, our own collective behavior is under scrutiny, while we hear an appeal to our sense of responsibility.

But does this work? At least the banks and other institutions where Reverend Billy, Savitri D., and the Stop Shopping Choir make their appearances seem to fear that it does. Usually it only takes a few minutes before the police show up, and Reverend Billy spends another night in custody.

The fact that such actions, especially in hyper-capitalistic cities like New York, are also a struggle for public space is shown by the frequency with which William Talen and Savitri D. are arrested—and not just on private property. Paradoxically, public space is often even more protected nowadays than semi public space. Occupy Wall Street successfully pitched its tents in Zuccotti Park, a so-called "privately-owned public space," but every excursion it made into Washington Square Park, which is a fully public space, was always ended by a massive police operation. Occupy London, which set up camp on the grounds of St. Paul's Cathedral, found itself in a similar situation.

Means and Ends

In the German-speaking world, the currently best known artistic-political group, whose reputation reaches far beyond theatre and art audiences, is the Zentrum für Politische Schönheit (Center for Political Beauty), or ZPS, with activist Philipp Ruch as its key figure.⁹⁶ ZPS projects tend to pull everyone who encounters them into their agonistic arenas. Whether we come across it in person or through the news, we have little choice but to react to it. Public manifestations of the Center's actions (among them the erection of a Holocaust memorial in front of the house of a prominent German right-wing politician) demand that viewers take a position which is far from simple to occupy, raising tough questions. Do we share these strategies of "radical humanism," as the Center calls it?⁹⁷ Is one exploitation being replaced by another here? Does the end justify the means? And isn't it all more complex? Is this approach too black-and-white?

In this respect, the work of the ZPS bears similarities with that of Santiago Sierra or Artur Żmijewski. The terms might be different, since the ZPS aims at unambiguously pointing out those accused of crimes against humanity (having a foot in the activism camp). But the strategy often is comparable (having the other foot in art's camp), as in the case when the ZPS offers a €25,000 reward for evidence that would lead to the conviction of one of the owners of arms manufacturer Krauss-Maffei Wegmann (*KMW*; 2012) in a move calculated to arouse both superficial disapproval and secret elation. Since participating in the arms trade itself—the actual ethical crime in question—is not punishable by law, the Center asked for proof of any other punishable offense. The real indictment, however, was the posters and the website bearing the names and faces of the KMW owners, in the style of "Wanted" notices from Westerns.

Legitimate critiques, surely, but are these legitimate measures? A later ZPS action which increased this same artistically productive ambiguity involved stealing the crosses from a memorial installation for the victims of the Berlin Wall next to the Reichstag, allegedly in order to bring them to the EU's external border, the site of a present-day wall and its victims. The criteria dilemma reached its temporary climax when the artivists saved the body of a refugee from the mass grave and buried it in Berlin—with all the theatrical ambiguity of the "as if."

A favorite tool of the Center is to play constantly with the distinction between fiction and truth to create uncertainty. How should we behave if we aren't even sure of the ground on which we stand? Is *The Federal Emergency Programme* (2014), which offers Syrian children for adoption, actually an initiative from the Minister for Family Affairs? Do the coffins belonging to the action *The Dead are Coming* (2015) really contain the bodies of drowned refugees? Is the online bounty system targeting neo-Nazis and right-wing extremists involved in the Chemnitz riots (*CSI: Chemnitz*, 2018) really a call for a manhunt?

Fake News

Such games with cleverly placed untruths have long been part of the artist-activist repertoire. A hoax is a prank in the form of a false report with the aim of luring the mass media onto a false trail and thus spreading a message as widely as possible. The real trick is that if it succeeds, it makes it into the news twice: first with the hoax itself and then again when the prank is uncovered. The act of unmasking is also what decisively separates this tactic from the fake news spread by Trump and his ilk. The aim of the artistic-activist hoax is enlightenment, not obfuscation.

The New York-based activist duo the Yes Men, consisting of Jacques Servin (pseudonym: Andy Bichlbaum) and Igor Vamos (Mike Bonanno), have mastered this strategy. Several documentaries and countless Internet videos show them posing as Exxon-Mobil representatives at a fossil fuel industry gathering to present candles made from oil extracted from the corpses of climate victims (2007), touting the *Acceptable Risk* standard, which states just how many deaths are acceptable in the pursuit of profit maximi-

The Yes Men: *Dow Does the Right Thing*

zation, at a banking conference (2005), or introducing spherical inflatable suits called *SurvivaBalls* that will make it easier for the managerial class to survive in the face of too-rapid climate change (2006). Their portfolio also includes fake websites of the World Trade Organization and George W. Bush (both 1999) and a legendary, yet unfortunately also fake, edition of the *New York Times* containing only good news (2008).

By far their most famous action, however, took place in 2004. It was the twentieth anniversary of the industrial disaster in Bhopal, India, which left thousands dead and hundreds of thousands more exposed to toxic chemicals. The Union Carbide group, which owned the factory at fault, denied responsibility; the victims were never even remotely adequately compensated.

Jude Finisterra, the spokesperson for Union Carbide's successor company Dow Chemical, seemed visibly nervous as he delivered a live announcement from Paris via a BBC World News newscaster. But this might have been due to the surprising content of his announcement: "Today is a great day for all of us at Dow and I think for millions of people around the world as well. ... Today I am very, very happy to announce that for the first time Dow is accepting full responsibility for the Bhopal catastrophe." To this end, Finisterra said, Union Carbide ("this nightmare for the world and this headache for Dow") would be completely liquidated and victims of the disaster would receive $12 billion in compensation.

But Finisterra was actually Yes Man Jacques Servin, who had managed to get one of the world's most famous news channels to fall for a fake identity. During the two hours it took for the fictional company spokesperson to be exposed, Dow Chemical's value on Wall Street fell by $2 billion. The news traveled around the world. When it became clear that it was a swindle, the news traveled around the world a second time with even greater reach. The media published around 600 articles on the subject in the USA alone. The Yes Men had rocketed the scandal back to the top of the public agenda. Dow Chemicals' rapid stock market crash acted as proof that the market does not necessarily reward ethically correct actions.

More often than not, however, the Yes Men engage in less hopeless struggles and support campaigns that strive for achievable change, using embarrassment and laughter to increase media pressure on companies or institutions that generate profits at the expense of people and the environment. For the Yes Men what is important is accessibility, elucidation and above all the encouragement of action. The Yes-Lab, set up in 2007 for this purpose, works to pass on the Yes Men's experience and methods to younger activists and students. While this includes things like sophisticated PR plans, the crucial elements (as with the Church of Stop Shopping or the Clown Army) are fun and humor. This, too, is a strategy that now has its own name: laughtivism.[98]

> Our general "theory of change" is that by using humor to bring underrepresented issues to large groups of people, or (more usually) to pile on to issues that are newly getting attention, we can "shift the spectrum of allies"—getting "passive opponents" (people on the other side of the issue, but only by default, who don't really care that much) to see the issue in a new light and become "passive allies," and possibly getting "passive allies" to become "active allies" (for this, they need to discover ways they can act on the issue at hand, which is one of the reasons a carefully constructed "reveal" release, pointing to ongoing initiatives of activist organizations, is so important). Humor is powerful, and the momentary deception we engage in is just there to add to the humor of the action, to make journalists (and hence readers) laugh. [99]

Forced Positionings

The Center for Political Beauty attempts a balancing act between art and activism by flanking the artistic ambiguity of its actions with clear activist formulations of goals and interpretations. The

Center for Political Beauty: *Federal Kindertransporte* (Montage)

DIE BUNDESFAMILIEN-MINISTERIN KOMMT!

fact that the note it usually strikes (in clear contrast to Reverend Billy and the Yes Men) is one of "aggressive humanism" is, however, ultimately part of an artistic strategy of ambiguity. For many, especially those who are in principle like-minded, this is perhaps the greatest provocation: the imposition of a morally demanded consent. The Center's self-styled heroic arrogance and propagandistic style (that calls to mind, more recently, climate activist groups such as Extinction Rebellion or The Last Generation) provoke many to object even when they actually want to agree. We don't get off the hook so easily when it comes to the social division of labor: the pressure to take a stance cannot simply be dissolved into superficial affection among sympathizers.

Works by the ZPS want to make withdrawal impossible. Broad inclusion takes place on the stage of the popular media, which for the Center is anything but a secondary playing field. As is the case for Christoph Schlingensief (who is frequently cited as a precursor for the ZPS, though their approach otherwise has little in common), news coverage is not a by-product, not just a place for documentation or critique, but a central element of the work. It is a space ripe for manipulation and play. The Center leaves as little as possible up to chance. They provide benevolent journalists with information, material, a specific interpretation, and a direction of attack, so that less sympathetic reporters and commentators will be unable to obscure the Center's own view. They set the stage so that when other actors take back the spotlight, an agonistic game can begin, where condemnation is followed by defense and defense by condemnation, across editorial borders between politics, feuilleton, and local news.

Theatre is a medium that does not merely endure contradictions between art and politics; it lives from them.

So far, the strategy has worked surprisingly well. Hardly any other artistic or activist action in recent years in Germany has managed to attract this much attention, far beyond the cultural pages.

And hardly any other action has been so successful at setting the agenda. At precisely the moment when the war in Syria had disappeared from the headlines, at precisely the moment when (before the summer of 2015) refugees had largely fallen from public view, at precisely the moment when no one was particularly interested in the German arms trade, journalists had no choice but to report on the actions of the ZPS. These actions offered opportunities that journalists often readily used to take up topics that had just been moved down the list of internal editorial priorities.

But it is not just the media that gets involved in performances by the Center for Political Beauty. Politicians, too, have to (or want to) take a stance; they are not only forced by the Center to react, they also use the Center's actions for their own agenda. And we too, the readers, TV viewers, Facebook and Twitter and Instagram users, we feel pressured to take a position.

Theatre is a medium that does not merely endure contradictions between art and politics; it lives from them. The performances of the ZPS play with precisely this productive, paradoxical ambiguity, interrupting reality with fictional breaks and contradictory images that shift perceptions and show the possibilities of action. This is their radical potential. The Center's pretentious motto "If not us, then who?" is a provocation both to the left and right, to activists and artists alike. It expresses the core of the Center's work: to create and perform on a stage on which contradictions are acted out, on which society emerges out of conflict, and with it a moment of radical imagination.

Milo Rau: *General Assembly*

THEATRE AS ASSEMBLY

It is a moment of truth when on the third day of *General Assembly* (2017, Schaubühne am Lehniner Platz, Berlin) Swiss writer and theatre director Milo Rau is called to the stage. Sixty delegates from all over the world have gathered to discuss "where we stand as a global community and what needs to be done—socially, ecologically, technologically, politically."[100] The goal is to create a "Charter for the 21st Century." When one of those assembled, a prominent supporter of Turkish president Recep Tayyip Erdoğan, flat-out denies the Armenian genocide perpetrated by the Ottoman Empire, things get loud. Emotions run high; the game has reached its limits. Some participants demand the speaker's expulsion. Others argue that a truly democratic discussion must be able to tolerate such opinions. Finally, Rau decides to expel the delinquent from the auditorium— only to call him back in a little later after further debate.

    This episode towards the end of an equally artistically and politically ambitious endeavor reveals much more than just classic democratic conflicts around the limits of freedom of speech. Suddenly the thin line becomes tangible that marks the proximity as well as the distance between theatre and politics. On the one hand, the inherent sociality of theatrical space makes it an ideal device for political experiments. On the other hand, the simultaneous presence of the symbolic and the factual that stands at the center of all socially engaged theatre becomes, in the realm of realpolitik, an essential problem. Theatre can transgress or blur the line dividing art and politics, playfully undermine it, or even penetrate it—but it can never ignore it. This demarcation, sometimes almost imperceptible, is one of the most productive challenges facing political theatre, as well as one of its most powerful tools.

Performative Assemblies

Trials delivering verdicts on artistic freedom, religion, and censorship; summits convened to wrestle with climate goals or cultural policy; parliaments that give a voice to the otherwise voiceless—theatre in recent years has become the setting for a wide variety of social assemblies that walk the tightrope between art and reality, a democratic arena built on a foundation of fantasy and imagination. By using theatre's ability to create temporary communities (its unique selling point as an artistic medium) defined by space, time, and shifting rules, this theatre not only reflects society, but also defines a container for trying out, analyzing, performing, representing, testing, pushing the limits of, and even reinventing social and political procedures.

> **Theatre can transgress or blur the line dividing art and politics, playfully undermine it, or even penetrate it— but it can never ignore it.**

The assembly, in the sense that the term has been used by, for example, Occupy Wall Street, is a core feature of an activism influenced by the traditions of anarchism. It marks out a zone for gathering, community-building, decision-making, and experimenting with how democracy can work. In this context, *assembly* refers to a meeting in which established hierarchies are abolished. In their place, a different approach to making decisions is not only tried out, but consistently put into practice. In this it aligns with Jean-Jacques Rousseau, for whom, in the words of philosopher Juliane Rebentisch, democracy "is above all collective self-government. Its model is therefore not the theatre, but the assembly—in other words, a setting in which, rather than one person demonstrating or playing at something for everyone else, everyone acts together."[101]

Nevertheless, assemblies have their own particular theatrical aesthetics. There is, for example, the striking use of hand signals, which function as a continuous performative commentary communicating consensus or dissensus. Or, in larger gatherings, the human microphone, a practice that turns the crowd into a chorus repeating each speech sentence by sentence, amplifying it both acoustically and symbolically. A performance that begins with the collective repetition of the speaker's standpoint, which therefore has to be taken seriously regardless of one's own individual opinion, at least in theory. In practice, the collective can also use the human mic as a show of force against someone who does not have the floor, drowning them out in unison.

Above all, however, it is sheer physical presence that gives such assemblies life, as philosopher Judith Butler emphasized in her (human mic-amplified) speech at Occupy Wall Street (2011):

> It matters that as bodies we arrive together in public. As bodies we suffer, we require food and shelter, and as bodies we require one another in dependency and desire. So this is a politics of the public body, the requirements of the body, its movement and its voice… . We sit and stand and move as the popular will, the one that electoral politics has forgotten and abandoned. But we are here, time and again, persisting, imagining the phrase, "we the people".[102]

For Butler, assemblies are political choreographies in which individual bodies cannot be viewed in isolation, but always and only in a lively relationship with other people, environment, and infrastructure.[103] Her analysis thus pays special attention to the performative potential of these gatherings.

The use of the term "performative" indicates in part a proximity to performance; however, since John L. Austin developed speech-act theory in the 1950s, it has also referred to the active potential of language and other cultural utterances to actually change reality—a statement that itself creates what it talks about (as with orders, promises, legal judgments, etc.).[104] In the early 1990s, Judith Butler radicalized this concept with her social and cultural definition of gender, in contrast to sex as a biological category. Gender is something that is *performed*, and produced, through speech and action. Reality is thus described as a construction solidified through ongoing repetition and quotation.[105]

In this sense, it is not only the theatricality of activist assemblies that gives them a performative dimension, it is first and foremost the fact that they are more than mere protests against existing forms of democracy. They create another reality, a lived alternative, simply by happening. They are not just a demand, they also constitute concrete action: "In the most ideal instances, an alliance begins to enact the social order it seeks to bring about by establishing its own modes of sociability."[106] This is precisely what is so often forgotten when movements like Occupy Wall Street are criticized for having no concrete demands. Such movements' effectiveness lies above all in the fact that their form, and the very way they take place, are proposals for a different democracy.

The risk, however, is to be content with just that, to romanticize the temporary and the fragile, when in fact after the peak of euphoria at the protest is not the time to rest on your laurels, as the philosopher Slavoj Žižek cautioned at Occupy Wall Street, in a (human-miked) speech echoing Brecht's warning that after the travails of the mountains come the travails of the plains:

> There is a danger. Don't fall in love with yourselves... . What matters is the day after, when we have to return to normal lives. Will

there be any changes then? I don't want you to remember these days ... like "Oh, we were young, and it was beautiful." ... There's a long road ahead. There are truly difficult questions that confront us. We know what we don't want. But what do we want? What social organization can replace capitalism? What type of new leaders do we want? ... The only thing I'm afraid of is that we'll someday just go home and then we'll meet once a year, drinking beer, and nostalgically remembering what a nice time we had here. Promise yourselves that this won't be the case.[107]

The theatre is not immune to the romanticization of self and authenticity, either. But because it longs for authenticity as much as it distrusts it, theatre can take complex intermediate positions and counter Rousseau's representational skepticism with a sophisticated both-and that unfolds theatre's unique potential—simultaneously artistic and political—by making it possible to participate and observe oneself from the outside at the same time. Where the Rousseauian assembly believes it can avoid representation, the theatrical assembly uses it to play an intricate game. Seen from this perspective, Brecht's V-effect is not an invention; it is the discovery of what it is that makes theatre theatre.

This specific quality—the simultaneity of the real and the fictional, of the authentic and the symbolic—is, with respect to the question of the political, theatre's real strength. At the same time, it is the line that separates activist assemblies from theatrical ones. And, not infrequently, it is a source of misunderstandings or even anger when a belief in authenticity encounters the paradox of a situation that is both real and fictitious.

Parliaments, Summits, Courtrooms

Though stylized, the concentric circles of structures and seating in the Sophiensæle, a theatre in Berlin, conjure the well-known parliamentary setup used by the United Nations General Assembly. The audience sits around an inner circle of standing desks; at their backs, unfurled flags adorn scaffolds of simple but precisely-cut wooden beams. Among the matters at hand are the right to self-determination and democratic reform, but also armed resistance and the War on Terror's legality. The representatives are a Tuareg from Azawad, a leader of the Kurdish Women's Movement in Rojava, speakers for the National Democratic Front of the Philippines and for the Tamil liberation movement in Sri Lanka, and two New York-based legal representatives of Guantanamo prisoners.

Since 2012, Dutch artist Jonas Staal's *New World Summit* has been one of the most consequent artistic answers to the challenges posed by participation and diversity. The summits open up alternative political spaces in the form of quasi-parliamentary assemblies that bring together people who are otherwise excluded from democratic discourse: representatives of organizations (mostly independence movements) that many countries list as terrorist groups. Jonas Staal holds that such lists are not least a tool of economic and geopolitical interests, an instrumentalization of the September 11, 2001 attacks which for many years took precedence over almost every other topic on Western political agendas.

The *New World Summit* gives rise to intense and touching moments in which political narratives can be heard that are otherwise mostly suppressed. A radical concept of democracy becomes tangible. But there are also disturbing moments of unease, contradiction, even anger. Obviously, political correctness is not one of the selection criteria for participating organizations. It is fair to assume that identifying with some of the groups, like the Kurdish Women's Movement, is easy enough for a liberal audience, while the same spectators may deem those that defend things like nationalism, violence, patriarchy, or rigid hierarchies in independence struggles rather unacceptable. The *New World Summit* welcomes very different organizations, giving no guidelines for how to evaluate them or relate to them. The one thing that is clear is the critique of Western democracies, the existence of which is based on the undemocratic, secret, and often—by their own standards—illegal exclusion of that which does not fit into the scheme. With art as its means, the summit asserts a site of progressive fantasy which is "more political than politics itself." A place "where the promise of an emancipatory, fundamental democracy can take shape."[108]

For Jonas Staal, such performative assemblies (in the sense of Judith Butler) harbor the potential for a new collectivity: a praxis that brings together art, theatre, performance, activism, and politics, which he calls *assemblism*.[109] On the one hand, these assemblies are artistic settings; on the other, they are directly connected with social and political movements, to which they offer the potential that belongs to their art: "We can help formulate the new campaigns, the new symbols, and the popular poetry needed to bolster the emergence of a radical collective imaginary."[110] It is precisely this production of images, of a visual language, that marks the relationship between the real and the symbolic in Jonas Staal's work—often in the form of a subtle game, as in the flags that surround the Berlin 2012 *New World Summit* outlined above, which are sorted by color and not by political or geographic similarity. The stage design of the summits, too, new with each iteration, is always artificial and unmistakably an artistic, experimental arrangement that openly displays its provisional character despite all the attention to detail.[111]

Because theatre longs for authenticity as much as it distrusts it, it can take complex intermediate positions.

It is no coincidence that the *New World Summit* has a particularly close relationship with the autonomous region of Rojava in northern Syria: its radical vision, following the model of a "stateless democracy" which rejects the nation-state as a colonial legacy and instead relies on local self-government, gender equality, and communal economy, aligns with Staal's ideas. And so there the temporary became a fragile permanent: commissioned by Rojava's autonomous government—made up of Kurds, Arabs, Syrian Christians, and all other ethnic groups living in the area—Staal and his team built a public, open parliament building, which was inaugurated in Derîk in April 2018. This parliament is equally a symbol of an almost utopian concept of society in a deeply precarious situation, threatened by war, as it is a concrete public space which any local group can use for political meetings and cultural events. It is "both a spatial manifesto of the Rojava Revolution, as well as a concrete space where its ideals are practiced on a day-to-day basis."[112]

General Assembly is not the first work by Milo Rau to use the theatre as a medium for a political assembly. In previous years, he staged a number of pieces that took the form of court cases; events that—like *The Congo Tribunal* (ongoing since 2015; documentary in 2017), which examines the ongoing Congo War and its crimes—could almost be textbook examples of an agonistic theatre, in the figurative sense of Chantal Mouffe's theory.

Rau designed *The Moscow Trials* (2013; documentary in 2014) as a theatrical means of reopening three traumatic court hearings held against Russian artists and curators: proceedings that tried the exhibitions *Caution! Religion* (2003) and *Forbidden Art* (2006), as well as the feminist punk-rock collective Pussy Riot (2012). Protagonists of the real-life cases, as well as other associated people, confronted one another in the setting of an intimate courtroom erected in Moscow's Sakharov Center. On one side, curators, artists, and critics fought for artistic freedom; on the other, journalists, Orthodox activists, and priests advocated for the primacy of religion. Nationalist member of parliament and TV presenter Maxim Shevtchenko (who later was also a delegate in *General Assembly*) handled the prosecution, while art historian and curator Ekaterina Degot led the defense. The makeup of the jury matched, to the extent possible, the political distribution of the country.

Jonas Staal: *New World Summit*

The *Moscow Trials* were a small assembly in a confined space. Though the documentary by the same name may have had a much larger audience, the central theatrical event, the core of the artistic and political happening, took place in the Sakharov Center, the actual location of the exhibition *Caution! Religion*, which was shut down in 2003 for allegedly inciting religious hatred. For three days it functioned both as a theatre and as a real space in which radically different opinions were exchanged in a way that had not been possible outside of an artistic setting for some time. In front of the audience, who were for the most part as personally involved as the performers, the jury ultimately decided in favor of art's innocence, with the smallest possible margin.

Alongside parliamentary constellations, court hearings are among the most popular dramaturgical and architectural models for a theatre of assembly.* Haus Bartleby, an interdisciplinary project

---

* Performance has borrowed from existing assembly formats beyond parliaments and court hearings, drawing on the concept of political parties, for example. Christoph Schlingensief's *Chance 2000* (1998) was founded by self-organized regional associations and supported by numerous local political candidates, and the party actually ran in the 1998 Bundestag election—however, it was for the most part perceived as an art project, both from within and without. By contrast, the forty-four-day durational performance *United Estonia* (2010), by Estonian theatre NO99, was conceived as a purely fictional production, but it was mistaken by many for a real populist political force. More than 7,500 people came to the closing event, and political analysts even predicted a possible share of twenty percent of the vote if the party were to actually form—while *Chance 2000* received barely more than 0.05 percent in the 1998 elections. Other artistic assemblies are based on game shows or reality TV competitions. One of the most impressive agonistic performances of recent years was *illumiNation* (2012) by Hungarian company Krétakör (conceived by Márton Gulyás and Árpád Schilling). For two days, as part of the seventh Berlin Biennale, debates ensued about which monument would

based in Berlin, organized *Capitalism Tribunal* (2016) at the Viennese theatre brut, in which over fifty scholars, activists, lawyers, and economists brought symbolic charges for approximately 500 alleged crimes committed in the name of European capitalism.[113] The Swiss performance artist Yan Duyvendak and the Catalan director Roger Bernat, in *Please, Continue (Hamlet)* (2014), dragged the Danish prince before a number of theatrical courts, each with different, real judges, prosecutors, and local juries, to try him for Polonius's murder. Croatian theatre directors Tea Tupajić and Petra Zanki positioned international theatre curators as defenders of art in *The Curators' Piece (A Trial Against Art)* (2011), thus pursuing an approach comparable to *A Crime Against Art* (2007), organized by artist Anton Vidokle and curator Tirdad Zolghadr with curators, artists, and art critics, as part of a Madrid art fair. And the list could go on.

Alongside parliamentary constellations, court hearings are among the most popular dramaturgical and architectural models for a theatre of assembly.

Such works are politically inspired by the civic People's Tribunal, organized by mathematician and philosopher Bertrand Russell in 1966, to investigate American war crimes in Vietnam. And artistically? Among other things, probably by Brecht's *Lehrstücke* (or learning plays), but also by the popular agitprop theatre of the early Soviet Union, which often took the form of court hearings. These latter works were sometimes so convincingly realistic that

---

best embody Hungarian national identity. These were often tumultuous and involved extensive participation from the audience, predominantly comprising Hungarian expats. The advisory board, made up of prominent politicians from the left to the far right, was not itself allowed to vote, but rather limited to advising the actual jury, which consisted of somewhat unsuspecting young Germans who had been placed through an unemployment initiative.

they stood in clear opposition to Brecht's dictum of distance. Walter Benjamin, who in 1926 happened to be present for such a production in a peasants' club in Moscow, shows in his *Moscow Diary* the extent to which they increasingly mingled reality and fiction; until, later, politics took the upper hand, and Stalinist show trials turned real courtrooms into (fake) theatre spaces.[114]

Not art *in* public space but art *as* public space (to use a distinction coined by curator Miwon Kwon): achieving this is perhaps political theatre's most urgent desire.[115] This public space does not have to be limited to the physical location of the performance, as has already been seen in examples such as the Yes Men or the Center for Political Beauty. Similarly, Milo Rau's court hearings expand the stage into the realm of the newsroom, where the discussion of politics and art continues. Such instrumentalization of the media goes well beyond standard PR work and is part of the artistic strategy.

Choreographer Erdem Gündüz's *Standing Man*, performed in June 2013 in Taksim Square in Istanbul, was a simple yet visually powerful example of this approach. At a time when the Turkish media was for the most part deadly silent about the protests against the demolition of Gezi Park and all public assemblies were being immediately dissolved, Gündüz stood in front of the statue of the Turkish state's founding father, Kemal Atatürk: a civil vigil memorializing a recent brutally dispersed gathering.[116] Gündüz's body, at first alone, then increasingly surrounded by others who shared in the endurance exercise and thus expanded to become a new assembly, became a symbol of resistance that, to use Butler's words again, "instates the body in the midst of the political field."[117] A body that, from afar, is reminiscent of other iconic images of resistance, above all the unknown man who stood in the way of the tanks on Tiananmen Square in Beijing in 1989.

There is a long tradition of theatres becoming sites for political assemblies, revolts, or even revolutions. This "is based on the observation of a certain resemblance between theatrical and political action, the assumption of a fundamental comparability of the boards actors tread, which stand for the world, with the political public sphere," as Oliver Marchart notes.[118]

The Brussels Revolution of 1830 began in the Théâtre de la Monnaie when, after a performance of the romantic-nationalist opera *The Mute Girl of Portici*, the audience called out for freedom and immediately began to march. The bourgeois audience identified with the mute and badly deceived fisher-girl onstage before them and raised the voice that she lacked. "Theatre had become the assembly," John Jordan writes, "and the spark, the site and event from which to launch an insurrection."[119]

The road led in the opposite direction in May 1968, when a different, but also thoroughly bourgeois audience—among them artists like Julian Beck and Judith Malina of New York City's Living Theater—left the streets of Paris to occupy the Odéon-Théâtre: "The action is not directed against any person or repertoire, but against a bourgeois culture and its theatrical representation."[120] Instead of performances, there were now meetings and discussions around the clock: "7 x 24 = 168 hours a week," as the theatre's dethroned director Jean-Louis Barrault noted.[121]

You can occupy theatres, or you can create new ones: as a memorial, as a utopia, or at least as a clear demand. The Plaza Theater in the Black Tent, which was built in early 2018 on Gwanghwamun Square in Seoul, capital city of South Korea, was one such symbol leveled against a corrupt government, the public erasure of poverty and unemployment, and increasingly oppressive censorship. The striking Black Tent was the contribution of a broad coalition of theatremakers to the demonstrations that took place every Saturday for months; it arose out of indignation at the reveal of the existence, long suspected, of a government blacklist, naming approximately 9,000 artists who were to be denied both any public funding and any appearance in state-subsidized venues.

Led by Lee Hae-Sung and Theatre Company Gorae, the Black Tent was a deliberately temporary performance site only used until President Park Geun-hye finally resigned and, shortly after, was sentenced to decades of imprisonment. Artists from all disciplines took part in the Black Tent project both financially and, above all, with numerous productions that were much more political than what could otherwise be seen in the country's major theatre spaces. It was important to close ranks with other sections of the population, including the survivors of a major ferry accident in 2014 that was never really cleared up and that claimed the lives of more than 300 victims, most of them young people. These artists also were showing solidarity with the unemployed, whose situation was kept largely under wraps; people affected by increasing poverty; and those suffering from the still-open wound left by the Japanese military forcing Korean women, cynically referred to with the euphemism "comfort women," into prostitution during the Second World War. For two months, despite noise and cold, the improvised theatre, supported by a broad artistic alliance, was not just a public space; it also worked towards a model of what theatre could and should be.[122]

Pre-enactments

While Staal's *New World Summit* represents those who are excluded from democratic or constitutional representation, Israeli arts and research group Public Movement's parliamentary project *Make Arts Policy!* put elected representatives in the spotlight.

For more than a decade, the group, originally founded by Dana Yahalomi and Omer Krieger and now led by just Yahalomi, has been investigating and staging political actions and public choreographies, forms of social organization, and public and secret rituals, which they themselves call "pre-enactments" of possible rituals of the future. One of their choreographic rituals in fact became part of the social protests in Israel in 2011. As Oliver Marchart writes, it thus turned out to be an "artistic anticipation of a political event to come":

> The pre-enactment presents itself as something like the pre-formance of a future political event. I would thus propose to use pre-enactment as a term for the artistic anticipation of a political event to come. But this event cannot be anticipated through simple extrapolation from well-known contemporary tendencies (as in the sense of role-playing science fiction scenarios). In the realm of politics, nobody can see what the future brings: it is unclear where and when social conflicts will break out. The artistic pre-enactment could, in this sense, be subsumed under the category of the rehearsal—the rehearsal of a future political event. To the extent that this event is unknown, however, the pre-enactment—with its entirely open outcome—cannot be a rehearsal of a determinate event; at best, it could be the rehearsal of an entirely indeterminate event, the event of the political. For this reason, it is perhaps preferable to think of pre-enactments not so much as rehearsals in the strict sense (as if the definite script of the future political event were available), than as training sessions. These sessions are there to produce the skills necessary to engage in the "actual thing", should it occur. In the latter sense, the pre-enactment is what in the world of classical ballet would be the exercise, the training of basic movements at the barre. It would be the warming up for something that may or may not occur. If it occurs, an artistic intervention on a cross-road may turn into a collective protest format of a social movement.[123]

In this vein, *Make Arts Policy!* was an attempt to initiate a different way of talking about cultural policy: a protocol-based choreography enacted by cultural politicians of all stripes, with cultural experts connected by video from an adjoining room and the audience, in the role of electoral representatives, in the plenary hall. The artistic interventions were subtle: switching politicians' chairs, employing colored cards to guide audience participation, musical interruptions, a dramaturgical frame composed of game-like rules. These small shifts established the theatrical context and distancing effect.

Because that's what it was all about: seeing political rituals with greater clarity and at the same time sharpening the differences between the cultural policies of different parties which are usually overlooked as all too specialized concerns. After all, almost everywhere, cultural budgets play at best a secondary role in the allocation of public funds; the actual framework of conditions for art and culture are determined in the other ministries.

So beyond the usual lip service, how important, then, is art—not only to society, but to the politicians who represent it? What role can, should, is it allowed to play? What is the relationship between politics and art? Is it acceptable for politics to delegate social tasks to art? In times of financial hardship, what is worth keeping? What can we do away with?

A first realization of *Make Arts Policy!* took place in Helsinki in 2014, amid the tense mood of Finnish parliamentary elections. Leading political representatives presented their proposals for cultural policy after the right-wing populist Finns Party (formerly True Finns) called for a radical cut in the arts budget. The German version, *Macht Kunst Politik!*, was realized two years later in Düsseldorf, capital of North Rhine-Westphalia, before the state elections at a time when almost all political debates were overshadowed and increasingly made more heated by the challenges posed by immigration and the influx of refugees.

However, whereas in Finland the participating politicians vigorously and militantly marked out their own positions and thus drew clear distinctions between themselves, in Düsseldorf they almost all emphasized the commonality of their efforts: their perceived op-

Rimini Protokoll: *World Climate Change Conference*

ponents were other governmental agencies, above all the Ministry of Finance, not the other parties—with the exception of the then still new far-right party Alternative for Germany (Alternative für Deutschland, AfD). As understandable as this pragmatic stance of consensus is, it nevertheless prevents cultural policy from becoming an arena for the public development of alternatives. Instead, it becomes purely a lobbyist's affair.

On the day of the event this was clear from early on: no agonistic, enthusiastic debate over different, clearly formulated agendas for cultural policy was about to emerge. Instead, time was wasted agreeing ceremoniously to dismiss the ideas of the right, while largely avoiding the formulation of alternative considerations or even visions. Only the AfD representative tried passionately to win the audience over to his conservative and at times reactionary ideas about culture.

In this way *Macht Kunst Politik!* offered insights that were not exactly pleasant. The goal of instigating change and opening up a view of what *might* be possible, at least for a moment, at least in the very limited field of cultural policy in North Rhine-Westphalia, was clearly not achieved. Seen from the perspective of a more conventional political theatre of representation, however, the project could be considered a success: it reflected the situation of cultural policy and made it visible through its theatrical framing. In other words, while *Make Arts Policy!* in Helsinki actually managed to initiate important disputes within the local art scene, *Macht Kunst Politik!* in Düsseldorf turned into an artist's representation of the existing situation rather than a pre-enactment of something that could be instead.

Two projects dedicated to the 2015 United Nations Climate Change Conference in Paris worked with a similar quasi-parliamentary setting: *World Climate Change Conference* (Rimini Protokoll) and *Théâtre des Négociations* (Bruno Latour and theatremaker Frédérique Aït-Touati).

Rimini Protokoll's *World Climate Change Conference* (2014) basically followed the procedure of the official *United Nations Framework Convention on Climate Change, 21st Conference of the Parties (COP 21)*. The 670 spectators stood for the 670 representatives of the 195 participating nations. They were assigned countries at random, and the attempt to understand and respect their designated nation's concrete situations, forces, limitations, fears and hopes, together with the limited time frame of the performance (three hours), led to results that were more pragmatic than utopian. In fact, they were mostly not much different from the results of the real climate conference, although in the theatrical version, the US somehow brought itself to increase funds for environmental protection all on its own. For Daniel Wetzel, co-director of the *World Climate Change Conference*, it was less about understanding UN processes than about identifying with one of the various positions: "You leave the piece having shared the space with 195 different perspectives."[124] This is reminiscent of Brecht's *Lehrstücke*, in which one is simultaneously observer and actor and thus learns to better understand the different positions without necessarily sharing their political and educational agendas.

Théâtre des Négociations by Latour and Aït-Touati with Philippe Quesne and raumlaborberlin took a far more critical view of the system behind the actual Climate Change Conference. The production at the Théâtre Nanterre-Amandiers revealed that the failure of the UN conference "is a consequence of questions of representation: the representation of the problems at issue and the representation of the various communities and living beings that coexist on earth." With 200 students from all over the world and many more observers, this simulation in a setting created by the architects' collective raumlaborberlin primarily intended to create visibility: "It was a question of making theatre a place where transparency and visibility prevailed, the opposite of negotiations behind closed doors," and thus "including in climate negotiations those entities directly impacted by global warming (indigenous peoples, young people, forests, oceans, endangered species, imperiled territories), but who have no possible way of having 'their' voices heard."[125]

In contrast to Rimini Protokoll, the viewers were largely released from the pragmatics of daily politics. Scientists suggested alternative explanatory models, artists developed new forms of representation, and numerous students from various disciplines sought out their own positions. As utopian as many of the approaches were, the focus was on concrete solutions for ending climate change.

While Rimini Protokoll's aim was to make the reasons behind the participating nations' differing negotiation tactics understandable and thus provide a somewhat realistic view of what is possible within this system, the *Théâtre des Négociations* opened up the freedom to renegotiate the rules of the game itself and forge new alliances, without at the same time straying too far from the original specifications: "Should our attempt be too close to existing negotiations, the experience would have resembled a classic re-enactment exercise. If too distant, it risked having no heuristic impact and being only an imaginary version of utopian negotiations."[126] Even if the agreement that was subsequently signed by all participating parties had no direct political influence, "it conveyed the slightly mad hopes of bringing about a new form of political representation by activating theatre's place through a new kind of political community, one not exclusively human, by including other actors from our common world."[127]

Like *Make Arts Policy!*, the *Théâtre des Négociations* draws its power from the concept of pre-enactment. Neither piece invents completely new settings; rather they use existing forms of political assembly and try to change their procedures, contents, compositions, and ethics. Their utopianism is pragmatic insofar as they imagine institutions that, while based on existing models, challenge and revolutionize them.

> **Such pragmatic utopianism imagines institutions that, while based on existing models, challenge and revolutionize them.**

Assembling Knowledge

Another playing field used by performative assemblies is the production and transfer of knowledge. Joseph Beuys' Free International College for Creativity and Interdisciplinary Research (1973–1988) was an early precedent. Some of the most prominent, but also the most carefully thought-out, recent examples come from theatre-maker Hannah Hurtzig and her Mobile Academy Berlin, with its "construction of public spaces in which narrative formats of conveying and dealing with knowledge are probed."[128] Theory and practice, content and form are inseparable at Hurtzig's *Market for Useful Knowledge and Non-Knowledge* (since 2004, formerly known as *Blackmarket*), where up to one hundred experts, divided in several rounds, sit in a large hall at small, carefully arranged tables, each illuminated by a light bulb, ready for one-on-one discussions which visitors can book for one euro as long as the seat is free.

Haggling over tickets for a one-on-one with your dream conversation partner is just as much a part of the Market's game (which has now taken place over thirty times in more than twenty cities), as is the high probability that you will end up seated across from someone else—matched with a fortune teller instead of the economics professor you had hoped for, or with a hairdresser instead of the world-famous choreographer. Facts, experiences, self-help, or just some insight into areas of knowledge of which you were formerly unaware all await. Those who are unable to get a seat at one of the small tables can watch the spectacle of murmurs from the edges of the arena and eavesdrop unnoticed on select conversations via headphones until, after thirty minutes, a gong sounds and the cards are reshuffled. Maybe it will work out this time; maybe you'll get your independent study with the undertaker.

Seen from without, a room of subdued conversations, an installation both restless and unsettling. And a strange feeling of seclusion, closeness, concentration when you are in the middle of it.

The Market is at once intimate and public. It is both an instructive, often very familiar dialogue and a theatrical setting; the result is a "hallucinated community college, in which learning and unlearning, knowing and not-knowing, life and survival strategies move between 'owners' in a non-institutional way. On this night, the transfer of knowledge as a communicative and performative act becomes a collectively whispered story of knowledge, taking place in the theatre, the original site of public debate."[129]

That knowledge can also be quite directly political was made clear by a Market that took place in the Colombian capital city of Bogotá in autumn 2019. After decades of civil war, in times of a shaky, tentative peace, the intention was to create a space dedicated to remembering that, at the same time, questions this remembering. It was therefore crucial that this Market had a partner from outside the cultural field: the Colombian Truth Commission (*La Comisión para el Esclarecimiento de la Verdad, la Convivencia y la No repetición*), whose mandate is to investigate and explain the recent armed conflict, and to promote the recognition and rights of individual and collective victims. Here, the *Market for Useful Knowledge* chose a thematic approach meant to enable people to talk to one another: the topic was oceans and rivers, which in Colombia function as important modes of transport and ecological habitats as well as sites of environmental disaster, alliances, bloody battles, and watery cemeteries.

Similar to Jonas Staal's parliament in Rojava, but also to Milo Rau's *Congo Tribunal*, this Market in the best case would develop an independent life of its own and become a model that the Truth Commission can use again in the future, with the aim of "addressing people from dramatically different milieus in such a way that they are brought together to actively participate in the public debate about coming to terms with the conflict."[130]

When Realism Becomes Reality

Milo Rau's *General Assembly*, described at the outset of this chapter, was also concerned with opening up new perspectives on the future using a different approach to existing parliamentary models:

> While Europe and the US are debating the modernization losers and underdogs, the proletariat and the shift to the right in their own countries, the General Assembly goes one step further with regard to the global reality of politics and economy, giving a voice to those who are underrepresented, who are not heard, the global Third Estate: labor immigrants, children and future generations, war victims, textile workers, miners, farmers, economic and climate refugees, the victims of the dawning ecocide, the oceans, the atmosphere, animals and plants.[131]

What distinguishes *General Assembly* as a pre-enactment from other examples of theatrical gatherings is Rau's artistic starting point as a theatre director who is wholeheartedly relying on aesthetic realism as an effective tool for generating experiences that are supposed to be cathartic and full of feeling. Emotional identification is the key to projects such as *Hate Radio* (2011), the reconstruction of the ominous work of the Hutu propaganda station RTLM, a driving force in the genocide of the Tutsi in 1994.

Rau's realism is effective and complex. As much as he believes in the basic artistic right to represent others, he is at the same time well aware of the ethical limits of speaking for others. Not only were all the actors themselves Tutsi and survivors of the war; the whole piece was developed collaboratively, in a process that, as Rau emphasizes, was not easy, as all of the actors were constantly being confronted with their own trauma.[132] Nancy Nkusi, for example, returned to her homeland for the first time to portray those who had incited her own family's murderers. This joint involvement in the development and playing of the piece makes clear what

Rau means by defining his artistic concern as "moving through a trauma with those involved in order to—only symbolically, of course [...]—put them in an active, performing role."[133]

The moral conviction that it would be unacceptable to let, for example, a German actor take on this role coincides with the artistic conviction that an authentic cast enables a more realistic performance. Milo Rau speaks of the "simultaneity of biographical or political and representational presence," which is at the center of most of his works.[134]

When the former journalist explains that "to work in the realm of realism just means to drag the real out of the shadow of documents and headlines, of 'the moment,' and into the light of truth and presence,"[135] the concept of "truth and presence" itself points to the central problem: ultimately, what *Hate Radio* does is condense large quantities of original material into two hours of theatre—and thereby becomes at least as much fiction as it is a container of documentary-style truth. Rau's belief that the material has to be edited in order to depict reality on a stage rightly dismisses the naive idea that extremely faithful re-enactment is a shortcut to historical truth. But in doing so he replaces the concept with the claim, no less problematic, that a work of art is capable of showing how it really was. Milo Rau performances are not meant to be read as one possible version of historical reality; they appear to unleash the force of an irresistible truth. *Hate Radio* is theatrical reportage that hides the struggle involved in making it, the dramaturgy, how it was put together, how gaps were filled. What remains is a perfect episode of propaganda radio that seems to be realer than any episode that actually happened.

In his essays, interviews, columns, and books, Rau develops a discourse impressive in its scope. In his performances themselves, however, he focuses more on the hearts in the audience than the minds. In more recent works such as *Five Easy Pieces* (2016), in which children present the case of pedophilic murderer Marc

Dutroux, he has brought this approach to perfection. With great virtuosity, he plays with the Brechtian V-effect, but only to lull the audience into a false sense of security and then, unexpectedly and all the more violently, to push them over the emotional cliff with clever manipulation. As much as Rau might indeed offer the protagonists of his works a moment of empowerment and participation, for the spectator there is little room for emancipation. Rau may be nearer to Brecht politically; aesthetically he is on the side of Stanislavski's overwhelming realism. In direct contradiction to Brecht's warning that the artistic representation of oppression merely repeats injustice and thus reproduces violence, Rau follows the Aristotelian injunctions to arouse pity and fear through mimetic representation.

It is important to keep the context of Rau's repertory œuvre in mind when considering the very different strand of his work that consists of court hearings, tribunals, and assemblies whose strict procedural dramaturgies leave both performers and audiences significantly more leeway. These projects can be seen as attempts to connect the two poles in Rau's work: the belief in therapeutic catharsis and the struggle for progressive political goals.

> **Rau may be nearer to Brecht politically; aesthetically he is on the side of Stanislavski's overwhelming realism.**

The double meaning of the word *acting*, which refers both to action and to performing onstage, plays a role, differently weighted, in all of the pre-enactment assemblies described here. It becomes problematic in conjunction with Rau's concept of "emancipation through submission."[136] In his repertory work, this can be seen as a question of aesthetic taste. In the context of politics it crosses a critical line.

This dilemma is also made clear in the *Ghent Manifesto*, which Rau and his colleagues published to mark the beginning of his tenure as intendant of NTGent, the Belgian national theatre in Ghent, in 2019: "Theatre is not a product, it is a production process. Research, castings, rehearsals and related debates must be publicly accessible."[137] But then why not make this process (including questions of hierarchies, authorship, the legitimacy of representation, and so on) visible—"accessible"—in the performance itself? Because it would contradict the striving for realism, for affective catharsis, for emotional identification. What it would make possible, however, would be a completely different sort of emancipation and self-empowerment. The danger is the same as in Brecht's diagnosis of Stanislavski: "He fights for the truth. He ends up creating a true guide for telling (natural) lies."[138]

> Theatre as an agonistic space thrives on public debate, on the clash of opposing positions. And it thrives on serious participation.

It is precisely this contradiction that made the discussions about the aforementioned denial of the Armenian genocide by AKP supporter Tuğrul Selmanoğlu the turning point of Rau's *General Assembly*. At this point, attention was focused not just on the case itself, but the entire artistic setup. The problem with "The first world parliament in the history of mankind"[139] was not the hubris of the undertaking, which is what gave the work its utopian quality in the first place, but rather the belief that this "world parliament" could be guided by invisible dramaturgical threads. While the agonistic (and at times antagonistic) spheres that Rau indeed repeatedly manages to create reflect his belief in an urgent democratic need for more open debate, the way he creates them follows a carefully planned-out dramaturgical logic, from rising action to climax.

In *General Assembly* the meta-discourse about both theatre and parliamentary politics was always present, but the extent to which the whole thing was staged was never clear. What was a directorial choice, what was anticipated—or even forced? To what extent was it possible to influence the course of events? How does reality come into its own within a realism over which a director does not want to give up control?

This dilemma of theatre reflects—as is so often the case—the dilemma of contemporary politics. The manipulative aspect of Rau's work is a major reason for its impressive success. Of all the examples mentioned, his assemblies and court hearings not only enjoy the widest media coverage and attract the largest audiences, they sometimes even enjoy measurable success in real political contexts. *The Congo Tribunal*, for example, led to a campaign aimed at establishing further tribunals in the country, supported by the Bar Association in the DRC, the International Court of Justice in The Hague, and others.[140] But even if politics always has an "affective dimension,"[141] the idea that the road to political emancipation could be paved by psychological manipulation remains a blatant contradiction.

Theatre as an agonistic space thrives on public debate, on the clash of opposing positions. And it thrives on serious participation, even if this is not always a pleasant experience. As Claire Bishop points out: participation in art should create a feeling of "unease and discomfort rather than belonging." All participants should be treated as "subject[s] of independent thought." This is the "essential prerequisite for political action."[142]

And so one could say that the unintended scandal at the end of *General Assembly*, paradoxically, did just that: by breaking the script, it turned those involved into "subjects of independent thought" and transformed a theatrical work into a political situation, into a real assembly. In response to the interjection "But it's theatre!" from the audience, the Turkish-born activist Aral Balkan replied: "For some of us this is not theatre, for some of us this is something that impacts our lives. And we are not here to be your actors."[143]

Theatre can re-enact, enact, or pre-enact assemblies. It can create spaces for analysis, reflection, imagination, or intervention. But the moment it becomes an actual assembly, realism ends and reality begins. With all its theatricality.

Public Movement: *Macht Kunst Politik!*

EPILOGUE

What kind of theatre do we need at a time when democracies are being dismantled, right-wing populism is on the rise worldwide, when social injustice continues to grow, wars are spreading, and the climate catastrophe requires all our attention?

We could conjure up worlds gone by, old solutions. We could insist that everything can be shown, said, and represented as it used to be. We could wish the audience back into the darkness or for an art in which the concepts of ethics and aesthetics are neatly separated, in which prosceniums and frames still guarantee autonomy.

Or we could understand present dangers as a mission for the theatre. Unclear circumstances are a rich breeding ground for art. Permanent learning by doing; no time to sit back and watch. "Start cooking, the recipe will follow!" advises Brian Eno.[144]

Precisely because optimistic forecasts are hard to come by at the moment, it does not help to bury our heads in the sand. The crisis of current social, political, and ecological systems is undoubtedly a threat, but it also holds an opportunity: to gain more terrain for democracy.[145] The world will be different. And so will art.

In this situation, we need a theatre in which agonistic confrontation is possible. A theatre which throws itself into necessary conflicts beyond its own walls, fists raised. A theatre that pulls its weight in the increasingly intractable struggles shaping politics and everyday life almost everywhere on Earth.

While neoliberalism has recently gone somewhat out of fashion as a panacea, the extreme right has perfidiously and with some finesse taken over anti-fascist philosopher and politician Antonio Gramsci's concept of cultural hegemony.[146] Gramsci describes how, in order to win elections, one must first struggle for cultural supremacy: with all the communicative means at our disposal—from classic newspapers to the comment sections of virtual social networks to meme production—public debates must be influenced massively and for such an extended period of time that the social discourse as a whole is changed and ideologically infiltrated. Electoral success itself is then only the final logical step. A gradual shift in what can be believed, said, or done, at the most basic level, must come first. As a response to the seductions of illiberal to right-wing demagogues, mere opposition is not enough. Standing up to them is important. Above all, however, other social narratives are needed: narratives that are both daring and relatable, truly progressive alternatives. We must create our own new images of the future and fight for social discourse. Political theatre can be a laboratory for developing, with radical imagination, such new narratives and testing them on a small scale. Like Jonas Staal, one can also call this counterpropaganda: "We should … begin to develop fact-based propaganda narratives of our own. New narratives about where we come from, who we are, and most of all, who we still can become."[147] It is not enough to refute the lies of others. The truth also needs new stories and images with which it can be spread.

> Above all other social narratives are needed. Narratives that are both daring and relatable: truly progressive alternatives.

The examples in this book show the manifold ways in which political theatre today—together with its audience—invents such narratives, such images, but also new forms of social coexistence. There is no short or long organum that we could simply follow. We are in a phase of experimentation, of finding out—as artists as well as spectators. But there are numerous approaches to artistic work and social commitment that make clear the potential of the encounter between art and political action.

What is needed is an art that is self-reflective but does not fall into the trap of pure self-referentiality. An art that does not take up political issues as heated clichés yet dares to take clear positions and endures both internal and external contradictions. An art that does not regard its knowledge of the contingency of our world as an excuse to leave everything to chance, but as a mission to counter the arbitrariness of life again and again with its own necessary designs. An art that not only demonstrates and criticizes the ills on this planet, but actively participates in making the world a better place, as corny as that may sound.

What theatre can contribute to this is its special competence in bringing people together in situations that are at once peculiarly real and fictional, actual and symbolic. In the paradoxical machine of theatre, we can be part of a social game and at the same time critically observe ourselves from the outside, while we are busy understanding the rules, negotiating them, changing them, or even trying out a completely different game.

It's that simple. And that complicated.

Notes

1 The quote (trans. Cory Tamler) is attributed to Karl Marx, Bertolt Brecht, and Vladimir Mayakovsky. Certainly, at least, the sentence can be found in Trotsky's writings: "Art, so it is said, is not a mirror, but a hammer: it does not reflect, it shapes." (Leon Trotsky, *Literature and Revolution*. Chicago: Haymarket Books, 2005 [Russian first edition 1924]. P. 120.).
2 Francis Fukuyama. *The End of History and the Last Man*. New York [u. a.]: Free Press [u. a.], 1992.
3 David Castle, "Hearts, Minds and Radical Democracy: Interview with Ernesto Laclau and Chantal Mouffe." *Red Pepper* (June 1998), under: https://www.redpepper.org.uk/hearts-minds-and-radical-democracy/ (accessed August 23, 2019).
4 Chantal Mouffe, *On the Political*. New York: Routledge, 2007. P. 52.
5 Ibid.
6 Heiner Müller, *Werke, Band 12: Gespräche 3*. Frankfurt/Main: Suhrkamp, 2008. P. 792.
7 Trans. Tamler.
8 The text is based on a novel by Josef Bierbichler. The title refers to a region in Bavaria but also translates to "middle rich," averagely wealthy.
9 Anta Helena Recke, "Oh baby, it's a white world." *Theater heute* 10 (2017): P. 51. *Quote trans. Tamler*.
10 Cited in *Mittelreich*, Münchener Kammerspiele, 2017. *Quote trans. Tamler*.
11 Cited in Matthias Dell, "Finde den Unterschied. Bierbichler-Stück nur mit Schwarzen" (Spot the Difference: Bierbichler's play, but with Black actors). *Spiegel Online* (October 23, 2017): http://www.spiegel.de/kultur/gesellschaft/mittelreich-an-den-muenchner-kammerspielen-diesmal-nur-mit-schwarzen-a-1174264.html (accessed August 23, 2019). *Quote trans. Tamler*.
12 Recke (2017). P. 49–51.
13 Eva-Elisabeth Fischer, "Schwarz allein reicht nicht" (Black alone is not enough). *Süddeutsche Zeitung* (October 14, 2017): https://www.sueddeutsche.de/kultur/schauspiel-nach-sepp-bierbichler-schwarz-allein-reicht-nicht-1.3707139 (accessed September 6, 2019). *Quote trans. Tamler*.
14 Gintersdorfer/Klaßen, project website "Das neue schwarze Denken –

Chefferie": https://www.gintersdorferklassen.org/projekte/chefferie/ (accessed August 23, 2019).

15 See Ernst Kantorowicz, *Die zwei Körper des Königs. Eine Studie zur politischen Theologie des Mittelalters*. Frankfurt/Main: Deutscher Taschenbuch Verlag, 1990 (1957).

16 See e.g. Claude Lefort, "Die Frage der Demokratie," in *Autonome Gesellschaft und libertäre Demokratie*, ed. Ulrich Rödel. Frankfurt/Main: Suhrkamp, 1990. P. 281–297.

17 See Jacques Derrida, "The Last of the Rogue States: The 'Democracy to Come,' Opening in Two Turns," in *South Atlantic Quarterly* 103 (2–3, 2004): P. 323–341.

18 See Paula Diehl, "Demokratische Repräsentation und ihre Krise," in *Aus Politik und Zeitgeschichte* (APuZ) 66 (2016): P. 40–42.

19 Bertolt Brecht, "Die dialektische Dramatik," in *Schriften: 1 (Werke/Bertolt Brecht. Vol. 21)*, ed. Werner Hecht. Berlin/Weimar: Aufbau Verlag and Frankfurt/Main: Suhrkamp, 1992. P. 435. *Quote trans. Tamler.*

20 Bertolt Brecht, *Brecht on Theatre: The Development of an Aesthetic*, ed. and trans. John Willett. New York: Hill and Wang, 1964. P. 189.

21 Quoted in Cornelia Niedermeier, "Der Ort, an dem Wirklichkeit anders vorkommt." *Der Standard* (June 28, 2002). *Quote trans. Tamler.*

22 Douglas Coupland, *Generation X: Tales for an Accelerated Culture*. New York: St. Martin's Press, 1991. P. 6.

23 Quoted in Florian Malzacher/Nadine Vollmer (eds.), "A Glossary of Life and Work," in *The Life and Work of Nature Theater*, ed. Florian Malzacher. Berlin: Alexander Verlag, 2019. P. 196.

24 "Bekloppte – das ist die Mehrheit. Christoph Schlingensief im Gespräch mit Henning Kober" (Crazy—that's the majority: Henning Kober interviews Christoph Schlingensief). *die tageszeitung* (June 8, 2002). P. 16. *Quote trans. Tamler.*

25 Hans-Thies Lehmann, *Postdramatic Theater*, trans. Karen Jürs-Munby. Oxon: Routledge, 2006. P. 17.

26 See Jacques Rancière, *The Politics of Aesthetics: The Distribution of the Sensible*. London: Continuum, 2004; and *The Emancipated Spectator*. London: Verso, 2009.

27 Quoted in Oliver Marchart, *Die politische Differenz (The Political Difference)*. Berlin: Suhrkamp, 2010. P. 13. *Quote trans. Tamler.*

28 Cf. et al. Derrida (2004).

29 Marchart (2010). P. 111. *Quote trans. Tamler.*

Notes

30   Jacques Rancière, "A Politics of Aesthetic Indetermination: An Interview with Frank Ruda and Jan Voelker," in *Everything is in Everything: Jacques Rancière Between Intellectual Emancipation and Aesthetic Education*, eds. Jason E. Smith and Annette Weisser. Pasadena: Art Center Graduate Press, 2011. P. 19.
31   Ibid. P. 33.
32   Hans-Thies Lehmann, "Wie politisch ist postdramatisches Theater?" (How political is postdramatic theatre?) in *Politisch Theater machen*, eds. Jan Deck/Angelika Sieburg. Bielefeld: Transcript, 2011. P. 40. Quote trans. Tamler.
33   Irene Albers/Anselm Franke, "Foreword," in *Animismus: Revisionen der Moderne*, eds. Albers/Franke. Berlin/Zurich: Diaphanes, 2016 (2012). P. 7. Quote trans. Tamler.
34   Bruno Latour, *Politics of Nature: How to Bring the Sciences Into Democracy*, trans. Catherine Porter. Cambridge: Harvard University Press, 2004.
35   Bruno Latour, *Reassembling the Social: An Introduction to Actor-Network-Theory*. London: Oxford University Press, 2005. P. 46.
36   See Jeroen Peeters, "Incidents and Incitements: Ecology and the Micropolitics of Spectatorship," in *Not Just a Mirror: Looking for the Political Theatre of Today*, ed. Florian Malzacher. Berlin: Alexander Verlag, 2015. P. 44–55.
37   Sibylle Peters, "Heterotopian Research and the Performative 'What if?': From the Salon of Destruction to the Animals of Manchester." 2019. Unpublished manuscript.
38   See, among others, Donna Haraway, *The Companion Species Manifesto: Dogs, People and Significant Otherness*. Chicago: Paradigm, 2003.
39   Live Art Development Agency, project website "MIF 2019: Animals of Manchester (including HUMANZ)": http://www.thisisliveart.co.uk/whats-on/mif-2019-animals-of-manchester-including-humanz (accessed August 23, 2019).
40   Alexander Kluge/Heiner Müller, *Ich bin ein Landvermesser. Gespräche. Neue Folge (I am a Surveyor: Conversations, New Episodes)*. Hamburg: Rotbuch, 1996. P. 95. Quote trans. Tamler.
41   Cited in David Hugendick, "Androidenliebe." https://www.zeit.de/kultur/2016-10/hiroshi-ishiguro-androiden-roboter-kuenstliche-intelligenz/komplettansicht (accessed February 1, 2020). Quote trans. Tamler.
42   Cf. Julia Farrington, "Case Study: Brett Bailey / Exhibit B," *Index on*

Censorship (May 15, 2019): https://www.indexoncensorship.org/2019/05/brett-bailey-exhibit-b/ (accessed January 15, 2020).

43   Cf. Abby Callard, "Emmett Till's Casket Goes to the Smithsonian," *Smithsonian Magazine* (November 2009): https://www.smithsonianmag.com/arts-culture/emmett-tills-casket-goes-to-the-smithsonian-144696940/ (accessed January 15, 2020).

44   Cf. Coco Fusco, "Censorship, Not the Painting, Must Go: On Dana Schutz's Image of Emmett Till," *Hyperallergic* (March 17, 2017): https://hyperallergic.com/368290/censorship-not-the-painting-must-go-on-dana-schutzs-image-of-emmett-till/ 2594450 (accessed January 15, 2020).

45   Quoted in Jens Kastner and Lea Susemichel, "Identitätspolitik ist erst der Anfang" (Identity politics is just the beginning), in *Identitätspolitiken: Konzepte und Kritiken in Geschichte und Gegenwart der Linken (Identity Politics: Concepts and Critiques in History and Today)*. Münster: Unrast Verlag, 2018. P. 7. *Quote trans. Tamler.*

46   For an insight into the relevance of such considerations in the German context see Peggy Piesche, "Politische Intersektionalität als Heilungsangebot" (Political Intersectionality as a Proposal for Healing). Heinrich Böll Stiftung (April 15, 2019): https://www.gwi-boell.de/de/2019/04/15/politische-intersektionalitaet-als-heilungsangebot (accessed January 15, 2020). *Quote trans. Tamler.*

47   Cf. Gayatri Chakravorty Spivak, "Subaltern Studies: Deconstructing Historiography? (1985)," in *The Spivak Reader*, eds. Donna Landry and Gerald MacLean. London: Routledge, 1996. P. 203–237.

48   Cf. Gayatri Chakravorty Spivak, *Other Asias*. Malden: Blackwell Publishing, 2008.

49   Cf. Julian Bruns, Kathrin Glösel, and Natascha Strobl, "Die Identitären – mehr als nur ein Internet-Phänomen" (The Identitarians: More than Just an Internet Phenomenon). *Bundeszentrale für politische Bildung* (January 26, 2017): http://www.bpb.de/politik/extremismus/rechtsextremismus/241438/die-identitaeren-mehr-als-nur-ein-internet-phaenomen (accessed January 15, 2020). *Quote trans. Tamler.*

50   Alternative für Deutschland, "§7.2 Leitkultur statt Multikulturalismus" (Dominant Culture instead of Multi-Culturalism). *Programm für Deutschland: Das Grundsatzprogramm der Alternative für Deutschland* (Langversion A4 Querformat). P. 47: https://www.afd.de/grundsatzprogramm (accessed January 15, 2020). *Quote trans. Tamler.*

51   Wolfgang Schütz, "Achille Mbembe: 'Identitätspolitik ist Opium für

Notes

das Volk'" (Identity Politics is the Opiate of the Masses). *Augsburger Allgemeine* (May 10, 2018): https://www.augsburger-allgemeine.de/kultur/Achille-Mbembe-Identitaetspolitik-ist-Opium-fuer-das-Volk-id51077901.html (accessed January 15, 2020). *Quote trans. Tamler.*

52 Mark Lilla, "The End of Identity Liberalism." *The New York Times* (November 18, 2016): https://www.nytimes.com/2016/11/20/opinion/sunday/the-end-of-identity-liberalism.html (accessed January 15, 2020).

53 Cf. Slavoj Žižek, et. al. "Mehr Selbstkritik, bitte!" (More Self-Criticism, Please!). *Neue Zürcher Zeitung* (February 3, 2017): https://www.nzz.ch/feuilleton/zukunft-nach-trump-mehr-selbstkritik-bitte-ld.143572 (accessed January 15, 2020). *Quote trans. Tamler.*

54 Daniel Binswanger and Stephanie Füssenich, "'Das Problem ist sicher nicht der Feminismus': Gespräch mit Didier Eribon" ("Feminism Certainly Isn't the Problem": An Interview with Didier Eribon). *Republik* (February 19, 2018): https://www.republik.ch/2018/02/19/interview-eribon-teil1 (accessed January 15, 2020). *Quote trans. Tamler.*

55 Sindre Bangstad/Torbjørn Tumyr Nilsen, "Thoughts on the Planetary: An interview with Achille Mbembe." *New Frame* (September 5, 2019): https://www.newframe.com/thoughts-on-the-planetary-an-interview-with-achille-mbembe/?sfns=mo&fbclid=IwAR2Lb_TAHWIYvYTak-vVkmQ3GBOwGOtKN6Q4j0rep-dCZuJ2bx4CHHRXQDyM (accessed January 15, 2020).

56 Victor Klemperer, *LTI: Notizbuch eines Philologen (Language of the Third Reich: A Philologist's Notebook)*. Leipzig: Reclam, 1980 (1947). P. 21. *Quote trans. Tamler.*

57 Einar Schleef, "Tagebuch 1999," in *Tagebuch 1999–2001: Berlin, Wien (Diaries 1999–2001: Berlin, Vienna)*, eds. Sandra Janßen and Winfried Menninghaus. Frankfurt/Main: Suhrkamp, 2009. P. 10. *Quote trans. Tamler.*

58 "Wenn ich in der Falle sitze, verhalte ich mich wie ein Künstler. Antanas Mockus im Gespräch mit Joanna Warsza" (When I'm trapped, I act like an artist: Antanas Mockus in conversation with Joanna Warsza) in *Forget Fear*, eds. Artur Żmijewski/Joanna Warsza. Köln: Verlag der Buchhandlung Walter König, 2012. P. 164–171. *Quote trans. Tamler.*

59 Ibid.

60 Cf. *Cultural Agents Reloaded: The Legacy of Antanas Mockus*, ed. Carlo Tognato. Cambridge, MA: Harvard University Press, 2017.

Notes

61 Wikipedia entry, Antanas Mockus: https://en.wikipedia.org/wiki/Antanas_Mockus (accessed August 23, 2019).
62 Augusto Boal, *Theatre of the Oppressed*, trans. Charles A. and Maria-Odilia Leal McBride and Emily Fryer. London: Pluto Press, 2000 (1979). P. 141.
63 See Julian Boal, "Behaving like Guerrillas, Wary of the Enemy: A Historical Perspective on the Theatre of the Oppressed," in Malzacher (2015), op. cit. 70–76.
64 Excerpt from *Bad*, quoted in *Sich fremd werden. Beiträge zu einer Poetik der Performance (Become Strange to Yourself: Contributions to a Poetics of Performance)*, ed. She She Pop. Berlin: Alexander Verlag, 2018. P. 38. Quote trans. Tamler.
65 Lisa Lucassen, "Wir sind einige von euch. She She Pop und ihr Publikum" (We are some of you: She She Pop and their audience) in She She Pop (2018), op. cit. 11. Quote trans. Tamler.
66 Ibid. P. 16.
67 Nora Sternfeld, *Das radikaldemokratische Museum (The Radical-Democratic Museum)*. Berlin, Boston: De Gruyter, 2018. P. 78. Quote trans. Tamler.
68 Claire Bishop, *Artificial Hells: Participatory Art and the Politics of Spectatorship*. London/New York: Verso, 2012. P. 2.
69 Ibid. P. 3.
70 Ibid. P. 2.
71 Quoted from *Enjoy Poverty* (film), 2008.
72 Pablo Helguera, *Education for Socially Engaged Art: A Materials and Techniques Handbook*. New York: Jorge Pinto Books, 2011. P. 62.
73 Ibid.
74 Irit Rogoff, "Looking Away: Participation in Visual Culture," in *After Criticism: New Responses to Art and Performance*, ed. Gavin Butt. Oxford: Blackwell Publishing, 2005. P. 117–134.
75 Mierle Laderman Ukeles, "Manifesto for Maintenance Art 1969!" (1969): https://pompeiicommitment.org/en/commitment/mierle-ladermanukeles-manifesto-for-maintenance-art-1969-proposal-for-an-exhibitioncare/#03 (accessed December 4, 2022).
76 Ibid.
77 "Eine Übung in Vertrauen. Edit Kaldor im Gespräch mit Florian Malzacher," in *The Power of Powerlessness*, ed. HAU Hebbel am Ufer. Berlin: HAU Hebbel am Ufer, 2015. P. 7. Quote trans. Tamler.

Notes

78 For a detailed account of this discourse see Eva Berendsen/Saba-Nur Cheema/Meron Mendel (eds.), *Triggerwarnung. Identitätspolitik zwischen Abwehr, Abschottung und Allianzen (Trigger Warning: Identity Politics Between Defense, Isolation, and Alliances)*. Berlin: Verbrecher Verlag, 2019.

79 See John Palfrey, *Safe Spaces, Brave Spaces: Diversity and Free Expression in Education*. Cambridge, MA: MIT Press, 2017.

80 Ann Liv Young, project website "Good Sherry": https://www.sophiensaele.com/produktionen.php?IDstueck=1800 (accessed August 23, 2019).

81 November 2018 at Sophiensæle during an appearance as part of the "Save Your Soul" festival.

82 In 2010, for example, the lights were turned off on Young at the behest of curator Klaus Biesenbach in New York's PS1 after a loud controversy with other artists in the audience. See Roslyn Sulcas, "Provocateur Returns to P.S. 1, but Not to Provoke." *The New York Times* (September 6, 2010): https://www.nytimes.com/2010/09/07/arts/design/07young.html (accessed August 23, 2019).

83 Helguera (2011), op. cit. 59.

84 Ilia Papatheodorou, "Wir sind niemand. Ersetzbarsein im Kollektiv" (We are Nobody: Replaceability in the Collective), in She She Pop (2018), op. cit. 47–48. *Quote trans. Tamler.*

85 Ibid. P. 66.

86 Lucassen in She She Pop (2018), op. cit. 7.

87 Dorothea von Hantelmann, "Auf dem Weg zu einem neuen Ritual. Der individualisierte Handlungsraum" (En route to a new ritual: the individualized space of action) in *Immersion. Magazin 2*, ed. Berliner Festspiele. Berlin: Verlag Theater der Zeit, 2018. P. 16–19. *Quote trans. Tamler.*

88 Allan Kaprow, *How to Make a Happening*. Brooklyn, NY: Primary Information, 2009: http://primaryinformation.org/files/allan-kaprow-how-to-make-a-happening.pdf (accessed August 23, 2019).

89 See Florian Malzacher, "Putting the Urinal back in the Restroom: The Symbolic and the Direct Power of Art and Activism," in *Truth is Concrete: A Handbook for Artistic Strategies in Real Politics*, eds. steirischer herbst/Florian Malzacher. Berlin: Sternberg Press, 2014. P. 12–25.

90 For a detailed analysis of the performance, see Christine Gaigg, "Non-Violence," in *Truth is Concrete*, eds. steirischer herbst/Malzacher. P. 04 ff.

91 See Yekaterina Samutsevich, "Punk," in *Truth is Concrete*, eds. steirischer herbst/Malzacher. P. 251 ff.

92 John Jordan, "Clowning," in *Truth is Concrete*, eds. steirischer herbst/ Malzacher. P. 247.
93 Ibid.
94 Ibid.
95 Billy Talen, "Preaching," in *Truth is Concrete*, eds. steirischer herbst/ Malzacher. P. 232.
96 See Florian Malzacher, "Aktivismus als Aufführung: Das agonistische Theater des Zentrum für Politische Schönheit" (Activism as Performance: The Agonistic Theatre of the Center for Political Beauty), in *Haltung als Handlung: Das Zentrum für Politische Schönheit (Attitude as Action: The Center for Political Beauty)*, eds. Miriam Rummel/Raimar Stange/Florian Waldvogel. Munich: edition metzel, 2018. P. 320–329.
97 Project website of the Center for Political Beauty: https://politicalbeauty.de (accessed September 9, 2019).
98 See Srđa Popović, "Laughtivism," in *Truth is Concrete*, eds. steirischer herbst/Malzacher. P. 120 ff.
99 Andy Bichlbaum on The Yes Men, "Becoming a Clown," in *Truth is Concrete*, eds. steirischer herbst/Malzacher. P. 169 ff.
100 International Institute of Political Murder (IIPM), project website "General Assembly/Weltparlament/Assemblée générale": http://international-institute.de/en/general-assembly-generalversammlung-assemblee-generale-2/ (accessed August 23, 2019).
101 Jörg Lauterbach, "Wie eine Philosophin das Drama der Demokratie erklärt" (How a Philosopher Explains the Drama of Democracy). *Die Welt* (January 26, 2018): https://www.welt.de/regionales/hamburg/article172879287/Lessing-Preis-Wie-eine-Philosophin-das-Drama-der-Demokratie-erklaert.html (accessed August 23, 2019). Quote trans. Tamler.
102 Judith Butler in the context of Occupy Wall Street at Washington Square Park: https://www.youtube.com/watch?v=rYfLZsb9by4 (accessed June 1, 2020).
103 Cf. Judith Butler, *Notes Toward a Performative Theory of Assembly*. Cambridge, MA: Harvard University, 2015.
104 John Langshaw Austin, *How to Do Things with Words: The William James Lectures delivered at Harvard University in 1955*. London [et. al.]: Oxford University Press, 1962.
105 Cf. Judith Butler, *Gender Trouble*. London: Routledge, 1990 and *Bodies That Matter: On the Discursive Limits of Sex*. London: Routledge, 1993.
106 Butler (2015), op. cit. 84.

Notes

107 Quoted in Slavoj Žižek, "Human Microphone," in steirischer herbst/Malzacher (2014), op. cit. 122–127.
108 Project website "New World Summit—About": http://newworldsummit.org/about/ (accessed August 23, 2019).
109 Jonas Staal, "Assemblism." *e-flux journal* 80 (March 2017): https://www.e-flux.com/journal/80/100465/assemblism/ (accessed August 23, 2019).
110 Ibid.
111 Other artistic assemblies by Jonas Staal include, for example, *Artist Organisations International* (2014, together with Joanna Warsza and Florian Malzacher), a congress of twenty very heterogeneous international artist organizations produced at Hebbel am Ufer in Berlin, or the three-day training camp *Training for the Future* (2019, together with Florian Malzacher) in the Jahrhunderthalle Bochum.
112 Jonas Staal, project website "New World Summit—Rojava": http://www.jonasstaal.nl/projects/new-world-summit-rojava/ (accessed August 23, 2019).
113 brut, project website "Das Kapitalismustribunal. Ist Kapitalismus ein Verbrechen?" (The Capitalism Trial: Is Capitalism a Crime?): https://brut-wien.at/de/Programm/Festivals-Projekte/Projekte/Das-Kapitalismustribunal (accessed August 23, 2019).
114 Cf. *Gerichtstheater: Drei sowjetische Agitgerichte (Court Theatre: Three Soviet Agit-Courts),* eds. Gianna Frölicher and Sylvia Sasse. Leipzig: Leipziger Literaturverlag, 2015.
115 Miwon Kwon, *One Place After Another: Site Specific Art and Locational Identity.* Cambridge/London: MIT Press, 2002.
116 Cf. Erdem Gündüz, "Standing Still," in steirischer herbst/Malzacher (2014), op. cit. 134 f.
117 Butler (2016), op. cit. 11.
118 Oliver Marchart, "Auf der Bühne des Politischen. Die Straße, das Theater und die politische Ästhetik des Erhabenen" (On the Stage of the Political: The street, the theatre, and the political aesthetics of the sublime): http://www.republicart.net/disc/publicum/marchart03_de.htm (accessed September 5, 2019). *Quote trans. Tamler.*
119 John Jordan, "Performing Against the Suicide Machine: Notes for a Future Which is Not What it Used To Be," in Malzacher (2015), op. cit. 106.
120 Quoted in http://www.republicart.net/disc/publicum/marchart03_de.htm (accessed September 5, 2019). *Quote trans. Tamler.*
121 Ibid.

Notes

122 Kee-Yoon Nahm, "Rebuilding the Public Theatre: The Black Tent Project in Gwanghwamun Square." *The Theatre Times* (February 12, 2017): https://thetheatretimes.com/rebuilding-public-theatre-black-tent-project-gwanghwamun-square/ (accessed August 23, 2019).

123 Oliver Marchart, "Public Movement: The Art of Preenactment," in Malzacher (2015), op. cit. 149 f. Trans. Wilfried Prantner.

124 Florian Malzacher, "Almost Like a Learning Play: Daniel Wetzel of Rimini Protokoll in a conversation with Florian Malzacher," in *Intermedial Performance and Politics in the Public Sphere*, eds. Katia Arfara/Aneta Mancewicz/Ralf Remshardt. Cham: Palgrave Macmillan, 2018. P. 198.

125 Frédérique Aït-Touati, "For a Speculative Policy: Bruno Latour & Nanterre-Amendier's *Le Théâtre des négociations/Make It Work*," in *Empty Stages, Crowded Flats: Performativity as Curatorial Strategy*, eds. Florian Malzacher/Joanna Warsza. Berlin: Alexander Verlag, 2017. P. 156.

126 Ibid.

127 Ibid. P. 157.

128 Kiosk Berlin, "Formats of the Public: Tulip House's installation projects": http://www.kiosk-berlin.de/englisch/tulip.htm (accessed June 20, 2021).

129 Mobile Akademie Berlin, "Schwarzmarkt für nützliches Wissen und Nicht-Wissen. Die halluzinierte Volkshochschule der Mobilen Akademie" (Black Market for Useful Knowledge and Non-Knowledge: The Mobile Academy's hallucinatory community college): http://www.mobileacademy-berlin.com/deutsch/2005/schwarzm.html (accessed September 30, 2019). *Quote trans. Tamler.*

130 Hannah Hurtzig in an e-mail to Florian Malzacher, March 5, 2019. *Quote trans. Tamler.*

131 Milo Rau/International Institute of Political Murder (IIPM), project website "General Assembly/Weltparlament/Assemblée générale": http://www.general-assembly.net/en/ (accessed August 23, 2019).

132 Milo Rau in an e-mail to Florian Malzacher, February 23, 2018.

133 Ibid. *Quote trans. Tamler.*

134 Ibid. *Quote trans. Tamler.*

135 Rolf Bossard/Milo Rau, "Buchenwald, Bukavu, Bochum. Was ist globaler Realismus? Milo Rau im Gespräch mit Rolf Bossart" (Buchenwald, Bukavu, Bochum: What is global realism? Milo Rau in conversation with Rolf Bossart). *Theater der Zeit* (2015). P. 28. *Quote trans. Tamler.*

136 Rau, e-mail, February 23, 2018. *Quote trans. Tamler.*

Notes

137 NTGent, "The Ghent manifesto": https://www.ntgent.be/en/manifest (accessed June 20, 2021).
138 Bertolt Brecht, "Stanislawski (2)." *Schriften [Ausgewählte Werke in sechs Bänden. 6th volume].* Frankfurt/Main: Suhrkamp, 1997. P. 262. Quote trans. Tamler.
139 Rau/IIPM, project website, "General Assembly/Weltparlament/Assemblée générale" op. cit.
140 Rau, e-mail, February 23, 2018.
141 Chantal Mouffe, "The *End of Politics* and the Challenge of Right-wing Populism," in *Populism and the Mirror of Democracy*, ed. Francisco Panizza. London [et. al.]: Verso, 2005. P. 35.
142 Claire Bishop, "Antagonism and Relational Aesthetics." *October* 110 (2004): P. 70, 77.
143 Quoted in Rau/IIPM, project website "General Assembly/Tagesordnung": http://www.general-assembly.net/tagesordnung/ (accessed August 23, 2019).
144 Quoted from Brian Eno's news on Twitter (February 9, 2016): https://twitter.com/dark_shark/status/697247873386172416 (accessed February 1, 2020).
145 See Chantal Mouffe, *For a Left Populism*. London: Verso, 2018.
146 See Florian Becker/Mario Candeias/Janek Niggemann/Anne Steckner (eds.), *Gramsci lesen: Einstiege in die Gefängnishefte (Reading Gramsci: Introductions to the Prison Notebooks)*. Hamburg: Argument, 2013.
147 Jonas Staal, *Steve Bannon: A Propaganda Retrospective*. Rotterdam: Het Nieuwe Instituut, 2018. P. 14.

Index of Names

Italicized page numbers refer to captions.

Agamben, Giorgio 36
Aït-Touati, Frédérique 126 ff.
Anderson, Laurie 96
Arias, Lola 32
Aristotle 133
Artaud, Antonin 27, 84
Atatürk, Mustafa Kemal 120
Austin, John L. 112
Back to Back Theatre 32
Badiou, Alain 36, 38
Bailey, Brett 46, 47 f.
Balkan, Aral 135
Barrault, Jean-Louis 121
Beck, Julian 121
Bel, Jérôme 33, *35*, 42
Benjamin, Walter 120
Berg, Lotte van den 67 f.
Bernat, Roger 119
Beuys, Joseph 75, 129
Bichlbaum, Andy *see* Jacques Servin
Bishop, Claire 68 ff., 135
Black, Hannah 48
Blair, Tony 11
Boal, Augusto 66 f.
Bohm, David 68
Brahms, Johannes 19
Brecht, Bertolt 7, 27 f., 65, 67, 72, 112 f., 119 f., 127, 133 f.
Brecht, Werner 33
Bright, Parker 61
Burden, Chris 72
Bush, George W. 14, 102

Butler, Judith 111 f., 115, 120
Castellucci, Romeo 49
Center for Political Beauty *see* Zentrum für Politische Schönheit (ZPS)
Church of Stop Shopping 93, *94 f.*, 96 f.
Clandestine Insurgent Rebel Clown Army (C.I.R.C.A.) 92 f., 103
Compagnie Création Ephémère 33
Compagnie de l'Oiseau-Mouche 33
Coupland, Douglas 29
Crenshaw, Kimberlé 50
Cyrus, Miley 23
D., Savitri 93, 97
Degot, Ekaterina 116
Derrida, Jacques 26, 37
Duchamp, Marcel 26
Dutroux, Marc 132 f.
Duyvendak, Yan 119
Eno, Brian 137
Erdoğan, Recep Tayyip 109
Eribon, Didier 54
Extinction Rebellion 106
Foucault, Michel 38
Frljić, Oliver 49, *51*
Fukuyama, Francis 11, 53
García, Rodrigo 49
Garzaner, Mario 33
Geun-hye, Park 122
Gintersdorfer, Monika 24

151

Index of Names

Gintersdorfer/Klaßen 24, 26, *30f.*
Gob Squad 29, 32
Gramsci, Antonio 138
Guerrilla Girls 55
Gulyás, Márton 118f.
Gündüz, Erdem 120
Habermas, Jürgen 12
Hae-Sung, Lee 122
Haider, Jörg 9
Hantelmann, Dorothea von 87
Haraway, Donna 40f.
Helguera, Pablo 70, 80
Heumann, Hauke 26
Hurtzig, Hannah 129
Ingvartsen, Mette 41
Ishiguro, Hiroshi 45
Jesurun, John 29
Jordan, John 92, 121
Kaegi, Stefan 42, 44
Kaldor, Edit 74f., *79*
Kantor, Tadeusz 41
Kaprow, Allan 84, 87
Kennedy, Susanne 44f.
Khrzhanovsky, Ilya 86f.
Klemperer, Victor 58
Kompanie Gorae 122
Krétakör 118f.
Krieger, Omer 122
Kwon, Miwon 120
Laclau, Ernesto 36
Landau, Lev Davidovich 86
Latour, Bruno 41, 126f.
Leadbitter, James 75, 78
Lefort, Claude 36
Lehmann, Hans-Thies 34, 39
Levine, Sherrie 20
Lilla, Mark 53
Maatwerk 33

Madonna 23
Mahler, Anna-Sophie 19
Malina, Judith 121
Marchart, Oliver 36, 38, 121, 123
Martens, Renzo 70, 72f.
Marx, Karl 7, 12, 64
Mbembe, Achille 53, 57f.
Meding, Julia*n 78, 80
Melle, Thomas 44f.
Mobile Academy Berlin 129f.
Mockus, Antanas 62, 63f.
Mori, Masahiro 44
Mouffe, Chantal 11f., 14, 36, 68, 116
Müller, Heiner 16f., 45
Nancy, Jean-Luc 36
Nikitin, Boris 78, *85*
Nkusi, Nancy 131
NO99 118
Paczensky, Achim von 33
Papatheodorou, Ilia 82
Peters, Sibylle 41f., *43*
Pollesch, René 29
Public Movement 122ff., *136*
Pussy Riot 91, 116
Quarantine 32
Quesne, Philippe 127
Rancière, Jacques 34, 36, 38f.
Rau, Milo *108*, 109, 116, 118, 120, 130ff.
raumlaborberlin 127
Rawls, John 12
Rebentisch, Juliane 111
Recke, Anta Helena *18*, 19ff.
Rimini Protokoll 32, 42, 44, *125*, 126ff.
Rogoff, Irit 73
Rosanvallon, Pierre 37

Index of Names

Rousseau, Jean-Jacques 110 f., 113
Ruch, Philipp 97
Russell, Bertrand 119
Shevtchenko, Yekaterina 91
Shevtchenko, Maxim L. 116
Schilling, Árpád 118
Schleef, Einar 60
Schlingensief, Christoph 8, 9 f., *13*, 33, 75, 106, 118
Schröder, Gerhard 11
Schüssel, Wolfgang 9
Schutz, Dana 48, 61
Sehgal, Tino 42
Selmanoğlu, Tuğrul 134
Servin, Jacques (pseudonym: Andy Bichlbaum) 99, *100 f.*, 102
She She Pop 29, 66 f., *71*, 81 ff.
Sherry *see* Ann Liv Young
Sierra, Santiago 70, 72 f., 98
Spivak, Gayatri Chakravorty 52
Staal, Jonas 114 ff., *117*, 130, 138
Stanislavski, Konstantin 84, 133 f.
Stengers, Isabelle 40
Sternfeld, Nora 67
Stöwhase, Helga 33
Sturtevant, Elaine 20
Talen, William (Billy) C. 93, *94 f.*, 96 f., 106
Tarnawa, Jozef 72
Teatr 21 3
TG Stan 92
The Last Generation 106
The Vacuum Cleaner *see* James Leadbitter

The Yes Men (Jacques Servin [Pseudonym: Andy Bichlbaum] and Igor Vamos [Mike Bonanno]) 99, *100 f.*, 102 f., 106, 120
Theater HORA 32 f., *35*
Theater Stap 33
Till, Emmett 48, 61
Trump, Donald 14, 53, 99
Tupajić, Tea 119
Ukeles, Mierle Laderman 73 f.
Vamos, Igor (pseudonym: Mike Bonanno) 99
Verhoeven, Dries 47 f.
Vidokle, Anton 119
Voina 92
Warner, Julian 23, *25*
Warsza, Joanna 63
Weber-Krebs, David 41
Wetzel, Daniel 127
Wouters, Jozef 41
Wyspiański, Stanisław 49
Yahalomi, Dana 122
Young, Ann Liv 77 f.
Zahn, Oliver 23, *25*
Zanki, Petra 119
Zentrum für Politische Schönheit (ZPS) 97 ff., 103, *104 f.*, 106 f., 120
Žižek, Slavoj 11, 54, 112
Żmijewski, Artur 72 f., 98
Zolghadr, Tirdad 119

Image credits

p. 8, 13: Stills from the film *Foreigners Out! Schlingensief's Container* (A 2002, director: Paul Poet, global distribution: Filmgalerie 451).
P. 8: Montage/Design: Oliver Neumann

p. 18: Judith Buss/Münchner Kammerspiele

p. 25: Holly Revell

p. 30/31, 85, 136: Robin Junicke/Impulse Theater Festival

p. 35: Hugo Glendinning

p. 43: Chris Payne

p. 46: BARAC UK (Black activists rising against cuts)

p. 51: Magda Hueckel

p. 62: Fernando Vergara/Courtesy of *El Tiempo*

p. 71: Benjamin Krieg

p. 79: Jean Lingen

p. 88: Joanna Warsza & Florian Malzacher

p. 94/95: Brandon O'Neill

p. 100/101: The Yes Men, still from the film *The Yes Men Fix the World* (2009)

p. 104/105: Zentrum für Politische Schönheit

p. 108: Daniel Seiffert

p. 117: Lidia Rossner/Berlin Biennale 7

p. 125: Benno Tobler

Acknowledgments

Sometime in 2011, in my work as a festival curator, it became increasingly clear that conversations with artists demonstrating in Tahir Square in Cairo, Zuccotti Park in New York, and Syntagma Square in Athens could no longer simply be about art as usual. More pressing questions became essential and remained so over the years to follow: What role does art play in social upheavals? How can artists help change the world? And what is the task of theatre?

I am grateful to all those progressive, politically engaged artists and activists whose actions, performances, and events I was able to attend as a guest, spectator, participant, or collaborator. They are too numerous to list here; many—by no means all—can be found in this book. It is dedicated to their courage, ingenuity, and perseverance.

The Art of Assembly is the result of an exchange with numerous artists, curators, and festival and production staff. A special space is occupied by my time at the festival steirischer herbst in Graz from 2006 to 2012, which culminated in the great joint adventure *Truth is concrete*, a 170-hour "24/7 marathon camp on political strategies in art and artistic strategies in politics." I will mention Veronica Kaup-Hasler, Kira Kirsch, Anne Faucheret, and Andreas R. Peternell by name, but I am thinking of the entire team at that time. To this day I continue to draw on the research and encounters in the context of this project, and so does this book.

The journey continued with numerous projects and collaborations, not least as part of the Impulse Theater Festival from 2013 to 2017, where we—especially Emily Keller, Dominik Müller, Felizitas Stilleke, and Nadine Vollmer—intensively searched for socially committed forms of theatre.

As representative of many conversations about art, politics, and activism in recent years, I would like to highlight those with Ulf

Acknowledgments

Aminde, Annie Dorsen, Vallejo Gantner, Alexander Karschnia, Oliver Marchart, Chantal Mouffe, Jonas Staal, and Nora Sternfeld.

Frank Hentschker, Director of the Martin E. Segal Theatre Center at The Graduate Center, City University of New York, initiated and made this English edition possible. I thank Cory Tamler for the careful translation and the publishing house Alexander Verlag—namely Alexander Wewerka, Antje Wewerka, and Christin Heinrichs-Lauer—for the many years of cooperation.

The fact that I grew up in a theatre family probably had an even more lasting influence on my view than my very formative studies at the Institute for Applied Theatre Studies in Giessen. For this—including all the behind-the-scenes and canteen insights—I would like to thank my mother Gabriela Badura, her husband and my friend Roland Bayer, my late father Werner W. Malzacher, and many of their colleagues.

Last but not least, I would like to thank Joanna Warsza: of course for many things, but in this case especially for numerous references to artists and works of art, for our conversations, our joint research and projects. I thank our son Lew—for the fact that he is there.

www.ingramcontent.com/pod-product-compliance
Lightning Source LLC
Chambersburg PA
CBHW072144160426
43197CB00012B/2233